How God Got Mary Pregnant
And why He needed her

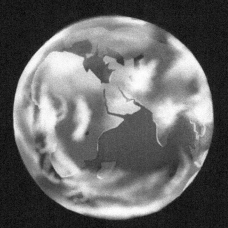

Jeremiah C. Southerman

How God Got Mary Pregnant
Copyright © 2024 by Jeremiah C. Southerman

All rights reserved. No part of this publication may be reproduced, distributed, or transmitted in any form or by any means, including photocopying, recording, or other electronic or mechanical methods, without the prior written permission of the author, except in the case of brief quotations embodied in critical reviews and certain other non-commercial uses permitted by copyright law.

Library of Congress Control Number: 2024915009

ISBN
978-1-961601-82-6 (Paperback)
978-1-961601-83-3 (eBook)

TABLE OF CONTENTS

Acknowledgements vii

Introduction ix

As Time has Passed 1

Imagery 5

God is: 1 20

God is: 2 29

God is: 3 31

John 1:1-14 33

The Obstacles 37

Dominion 67

So what is God Doing About It? 77

Abraham 83

Ok, so what? 98

ACKNOWLEDGEMENTS

I want to first thank The Holy Spirit for meeting me where I was. He says; "seek and you shall find," and that "He rewards them that diligently seek Him." And that "He is our teacher". Neither will He let you down …so, seek.

And

I want to thank my wife, she has been most helpful and supportive on this project.

And

The bulk of this book I got directly from the Holy Spirit during my own time in the Word. However, there are teachers out there God lead me to which confirmed and many times added to what I was "seeing darkly". I have to thank them for following the call of God on their lives. I will not name any since this is my first book, I do not know if any would want acknowledgment from someone such as I who will not conform to denominational standards as some of them do. Some I am sure will be in agreement with my teaching, but without having permission I will thank them anonymously.

INTRODUCTION

As a kid, my religious training was at a deeper level than the average kid growing up in the "Bible belt", even those who went to schools owned by churches or went on to Christian colleges. The reason for my depth of knowledge was the fact that I was in a Christian cult. That made me different and different brought questions, especially from the arrogant religious folks who's preacher had made them feel that they knew everything and anyone not part of that denomination was deceived. We in our cult/church were trained to... **"be ready always to give an answer to every man that asketh you a reason of the hope that is in you... (I Peter 3:15).** Studying the Bible brought answers. Later in life I walked away from the cult to find out if mainstream denominations had the answers to the questions that my raising had not provided. While they had some of the answers (more than my cult) that I wanted and needed, they did not have near enough. What I did find is that all denominations, have a form of religion in the name of God, but overall lack, as a whole real Godliness. Not each member, many try to walk Godly but the lack from the mainstream pulpits are little help to these folks. Frustratingly, I found much of it to be religion "of men". Note what God thinks of man's religion in I Samuel 5:3-4- **And when they arose early on the morrow morning, behold, Dagon was fallen upon his face to the ground before the ark of the LORD; and the head of Dagon and**

both the palms of his hands were cut off. This dagon was an idol of the pagan Philistines. By the fact that God made the carved image of dagon bow before Him is a good imagery lesson showing that man's ideas will someday bow the knee to God. God wants nothing to do with anything we can think up as religious rules, practices, beliefs, or so on (represented by the removal of dagon's *head*, in the above verse). In addition, He wants nothing to do with anything we build with our efforts or our hands (represented by the removal of dagon's *hands*, in the above verse). Sadly, too many churches have too many doctrines built on man's thinking (our *heads*), And most of our programs that the churches often get volunteers to do the *hands* on parts to save money, which use up few dedicated members lives to create the ideas that came from the shepherds *heads*, and or our mega churches that tend to draw us in originate in our *head* and are built with man's *hands*. Anything that *we* come up with is unacceptable to God and His perfect standard.

Later I walked away from all religion for I was done with the self-serving interpretations of men that live off the backs of the people. The Bible held the truth I was searching for that was able to set me free. As I walked away from religion, I was walking into God's open arms. What follows in this book is a small taste of things I have since discovered.

As an author I feel I am lacking, as a teacher I can hold my own, so I offer my apologies in advance for gutting the English language for you higher educated readers that consume poetry for entertainment and inspiration. If you are one of those, maybe you can find enough books by R. C. Sproul to scratch all your itches. I liked Mr. Sproul. I listened to him many times, but his vocabulary and mine are polar opposites. Now if you find, say, Phil Robertson more to your liking, then you will not have trouble accepting me. I am just a simple man that has an above average passion for The Word of God (*even amongst some preachers*). For 10 years I put as many as 50 hours per week into my Bible consumption. I found that much of what is being taught from the pulpits is a self-serving-carnal-minded-distortion of what God, who is a Spirit, is actually saying to humanity. The reason for this is that it sells. Our carnal minds easily understand carnal things and the carnal interpretations of what is actually a spiritual book. The idea is to tell the potential buyer what they can easily understand, make them feel good about themselves, and they will most likely buy the doctrine you or your denomination promoting. Religion is an INDUSTRY. What God gave mankind as an instruction book the Holy Bible, men made a religion out of later. When God through Jesus death brought and end to the only religion He himself ever sanctioned you can bet the next day the leaders of the Jews was figuring out how to sew that temple curtain back together that separated common folks from the holy of Holies. Because they had learned how to make money. It boils down to power over the people by brainwashing them to serve the cause, if the people do not actually get the total image set forth in God's book then they out of a good heart and soul give service to a religion that has a form of Godliness, even at the expense of their own lives. The newest religion on earth is the climate change religion. Its hard to control people at by force, communism has proved that time and again, but it easy to control sheepeople if you get their mind at a young age.

Also, all of my scripture references are from the King James Version, as most reputable teachers use.

AS TIME HAS PASSED

I have come to understand the answer to a question I discussed years ago with a preacher who had just spent a week or so in a doctrinal seminar. The preachers there had discussed the question of how did Mary get pregnant? At the time, I was comfortable with my answer to that question. However, after years of consuming the Bible, one day I realized the preachers had a deeper question after all, and the thinking I was so comfortable with in my twenties was not correct. My answer to the question at that time was either,#1) "No problem Mr. Preacher man, God just spoke and said, Mary be pregnant," the same way He spoke the universe into being by saying, "Light be" and light was. Or,#2) God sent the angel down to deposit Holy sperm in her womb and she was pregnant (no sex in the plan). Simple, right? However, when I got more of the picture I realized there was a problem with those two explanations, such as the following. It was easy for God to command His will when He and His will was all there was to factor in (*like 500 trillion years ago*). That changed when He create other life forms and gave them free will. He couldn't just say, "Mary be pregnant" because He had to consider Mary and whether she wanted to be pregnant. What if no female on earth wanted to be pregnant with a supernatural baby? Was God going to violate free will? I think not. If He were going to violate free will, then why did He not stop Adam from going to the wrong tree? In case the thought just crossed your mind because you have been taught wrong doctrine that *"God is in charge, God is in control, Its all part of God's plan"*. That filth is hog wash, sorry you drank it up in your ignorance, disgusting thought huh? I plan to help you out of part of your ignorance in this book.

In this book, we will also explore the person with the name of "Word." Strange name, you think? Word was alive long before He was conceived in Mary's womb and born to live a human life. We will discuss why He was named Word, why He became flesh, and the mechanics of how He did it. In addition, we will discuss why I keep capitalizing "Him" each time I bring Him up. For the Christian reader you already know who He is, and why He had to die. If not, then you are about to learn (even if you think you know you are about to learn something), for I almost bet you, fellow Christian, that you have not heard how God did it. One reason you have not heard is that this truth is not all important to the great commission (i. e. going into the entire world and preaching the gospel to every person). Therefore, preachers have no big reason to hone in on such details. However, for the person who desires to know God and the Bible, it is interesting and important. Student or not, believe me, you will learn from what you are about to read.

We will explore why it is that today you and I have it easy. Easy in that we can just hear the message of the gospel and if you believe it, say a few words, specifically, these words- **That if thou shalt confess with thy mouth the Lord Jesus, and shalt believe in thine heart that God hath raised him from the dead, thou shalt be saved. For with the heart man believeth unto righteousness; and with the mouth confession is made unto salvation (Romans 10:9-10).** Notice that it is a two-part deal; you must confess with your mouth (step one), and believe with your heart (step two). There are people who argue against coerced, manipulated confessions of salvation. They have a point, but I am not going there in this book. I will say this: just mean it when you say it. When you say these words, there will be a change inside you. Why? Because, God is a Spirit and He operates in that spirit realm primarily, and interacts with this realm only, because He loves us so much. When your mind comes to the point that it believes the gospel about Jesus our spirits become connected to that

How God Got Mary Pregnant

Spiritual realm that we do not touch with our five physical senses. Because what is happening is spiritual, it happens on the inside of us. It is not just a warm fuzzy feeling "felt" by your emotions. This means it is *not* emotional (*note the emphasis*), Your emotions will show it and feel it, but they did not cause it. Unlike a sappy old movie where ten minutes later your emotions are back to normal, the change is a spiritual one deeper than emotions. Your brainwashed polluted mind may come back to fight your emotions and tell you it was nothing more than something like a sappy old movie. That is where a foundation in the Bible comes in real handy. Nor is the change mental, so you may not think very differently at first. Jesus told Nicodemus in **John 3:6- that which is spirit is spirit and that which is flesh is flesh.** The two may never meet, and sadly that is where many churches and church members are stuck. Stuck in dead doctrine formed not from what the Bible actually says but a denominational handbook tells them to think. (*I've been there done that*) If we consume the Bible and live as Jesus taught us, the flesh will feel the positive effects of having a living spirit inside us. Unlike many religious people teach what is going on in the world today is not God's will; they are trying to marry their silly doctrine to world events, while maintaining Him as Lord. We will see how it got this way, what has been done about it, and how it can (*if you allow it*) affect you today.

I need to set the stage on some basics so that you can better understand what I am sharing, especially for the reader who is new to the Bible or has not spent as much time in it as some of the older Christians. We (at least the English speaking people) tend to study subjects based on groupings of words or word association. While this is not bad and it does us good, it is not the end of knowledge on the subject. We do not necessarily learn best by that method, because it disappears from our memory too easy. Unfortunately, many of us study the Bible that way. Most of us have heard the saying, "A picture is worth a thousand words". We know that our brain assimilates knowledge best if it can associate an image with the information. People who compete in memory competitions will tell you they always associate an image or picture with the items they are required to remember during the competition. When the list becomes long, the competitors begin to spin a story (much like a parable) out of the items so they can remember those items. God knows this as well, of course, so He teaches in imagery. Jesus taught in parable form for that same reason. Just as an example, if I say "cow", there is a good chance the image that just came to your mind was a four-legged cow eating grass................ *intentional pause here,....................you are suppose to be imagining a cow right now............* Maybe you just thought of a black and white Holstein, or a brown jersey, or a black Angus. One thing very few of you, if any, did was imagined the letters, c.o.w. In the Bible God used lasting images that would endure technology, political, and cultural changes. He used things like seasons, trees, plants, weather, and the basics of human life.

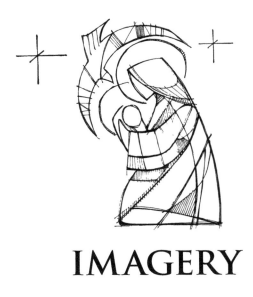

IMAGERY

What is imagery and why is it important?

Imagery is the tool the Holy Ghost uses most often to teach me. If the term "imagery" is new to you, it differs from images. Images are something you can see with your eye or walk up to and touch, such as a photograph or wall hanging. We form an image in our minds as we hear words, but when someone interprets those words, by explaining what image they want or need us to form in our mind they are manipulating the imagery you will "see". Our mind will draw/form an image influenced by them. For instance, in the example of the cow above, I did not manipulate your image until I started naming breeds and their colors. Once I did, your mind began to "go" in the direction of one of three choices I laid out. If you are a cattle farmer or live close to one that raises the Charolais breed, then your mind is already "indoctrinated" with the image of a creamy white cow and my "influence" had little or no effect on your thinking. Religion gets much of its success by manipulating the images your mind forms very early in your Christian walk. To combat this, we should consume vast amounts of the Bible as soon as we begin to have interest in spiritual issues. Imagery is something the Bible says without coming straight out and saying it. Imagery is kind of like reading between the lines. Obviously, there are specific commands, or "non-imagery", statements in the Bible. An example of a non-imagery teaching is in Exodus 20:15, where we read a statement, **"Thou shalt not steal"**. That is simple, to the point, no thinking required, nothing abstract. You do not have to read other parts of the Bible to understand that stealing is a sin. You do not have to read other parts of the Bible to understand what stealing is. There is no double meaning or deeper meaning in that verse. The point is clear: Do not take what is not yours. Imagery on the other hand, is more abstract. Imagery is not like a painting, a statue, or a bust of a famous person. To teach you what I mean about "imagery" here are he lyrics to a song, <u>Rose in Paradise</u> this was sung by Waylon Jennings:

She was a flower for the takin', Her beauty cut just like a knife…He was a banker from Macon, Swore he'd love her all his life…Bought her a mansion on a mountain With a formal garden and a lot a land…But paradise became her prison, That Georgia banker was a jealous man! Every time he'd talk about her, You could see the fire in his eyes…..He'd say,"I would walk through Hell on Sunday, To keep my Rose in Paradise…"He hired a man to tend the garden, Keep an eye on her while he was gone..Some say they ran away together… Some say that gardener left alone…Now the banker is an old man…That mansion's cum-ble-ing down…He sits all day and stares at the garden…Not a trace of her was ever found…Every time he talks about her, You can see the fire in his eyes. He'd say,"I would walk through Hell on Sunday, To keep my Rose in Paradise…."Now there's a rose out in the garden…Its beauty cuts just like a knife…They say that it even grows in the winter time…And blooms in the dead of the night…

In the song he never said the husband killed her, or why the husband felt justified for killing her, nor what he did with her body. There is no "thou shalt not steal" statement in the image put forth in the song. In other words there is not statement saying the banker got so jealous he killed her and buried her body in the rose garden. But it is clear once you see it you can't un-see it, that is what the story (i. e. imagery) of the song is telling us. It is that way with scripture on the first reading, we normally will not get the full image. That is why it helps us to "consume", or read repeatedly, the Scriptures so that we can bypass the "carnal mind" and begin to see the spiritual "image" embedded there.

Let's use the historical figure Galileo as another teaching example. The image he had of how the solar system worked was correct. In his case this was not an abstract image like the servant on horseback, (coming up in a couple pages) the solar system was out there for any to see if they looked long enough to study out the truth and not just accept the popular doctrine. He lived in a time when the official "doctrine" was that the sun rotated around the earth. If you did not study the patterns of the sun, moon, other planets, and stars enough, the official "doctrine" would seem correct. The normal way of thinking would have been something like this: "The sun comes up in the east, sets in the west, and the people that seem to be someone among us (the Catholic Church, in that case) tells us that is what is happening, so it is settled." "Therefore, I being a little uneducated *sheepeople*, believe their doctrine about the solar system." However, if you spent some time becoming more intimate with how the solar system actually works and get some help with your interpretation of what you are seeing (in Galileo's case the help came from a telescope), then you have a better understanding how the solar system works (you have truth) of what is out there. Today, we do not question that basic part of how the solar system works, but back then, humanity was ignorant of that. Therefore, the accepted opinion was the one with the loudest voice (the mega church with the most money for media would be one way to look at it today). With the help Galileo got through the telescope, he was able to "see" what he could not see or understand before. It works the same with your Bible. Our carnal/physical minds that receive information via carnal/physical senses needs help with spiritual concepts. With the help you get by reading scripture over and over, combined with the desire to learn truth and not just accept what self-serving religious brokers have told you, you will find that many a doctrine is wrong. I guess "wrong" sounds harsh and judgmental, so I should say the doctrine is "incomplete", or "shallow". I say incomplete because many doctrines fit what the unaided, carnal "eyes of our understanding" see on the surface. You will find this to be true when one digs deep and becomes more intimate with the spiritual concepts. In

Jeremiah C. Southerman

addition, one must ask God for help (God will become our "telescope" in this case). He said He would send us a Helper (the Holy Ghost- John 14:26-) to help us in all things and when you receive Him, allow yourself to flow in the help He gives, don't fight Him or resist what you may not, most likely will not understand. He becomes our telescope so that we can see what an unaided, carnal eye/mind cannot. Let's look at an example of an imagery teaching God inspired King Solomon to write:- **There is an evil *which* I have seen under the sun, as an error *which* proceedeth from the ruler: Folly is set in great dignity, and the rich sit in low place. I have seen servants upon horses, and princes walking as servants upon the earth (Ecc. 10:5-7).** A quick, shallow glance at this verse gives the image of a pauper, a vagabond, a poor uneducated servant, riding the horse while the prince (a child of a king, born into royalty) an educated chap, is being forced to walk because the servant "chap" has somehow pulled this off, hoodwinked the prince, or over-powered the prince or something. That interpretation is not wrong, but neither is it right; it is "shallow", or carnal, because there is much more to it. The Bible, is a big, deep, spiritual book and we Christians do not tap its depths (sadly, too many of us do not try). The spiritual lesson that God was having Solomon write down is this: the horse is our flesh body that carries us through the Adamic domain for approximately 70 years. The servant is our soul that serves our spirit. Our spirit is the prince, born of royalty (*you are born of royalty if you have done the Romans 10:9-10 thing*), royalty that should be in charge, and/or, should be riding/controlling the horse. If that explanation did not make sense, it should by the time we get to the end of the book. This theme, repeated in other places in the Bible, is foundational to our understanding of the Bible. Let's go look at some foundation for the things I want you to "see" (understand) resulting from my studies.

The reason I want to do this is that if you do not understand whom and what God is and what He is doing on earth, you will not understand other basic lessons taught in scripture. You will not understand why Mary got pregnant with this Word person, who this Word person is, why He came to earth, and why He had to die. This is where hunting other parts of scripture adds to the image of whatever it is you are learning from scripture. To get the entire image from the Bible, one must consume the entire Bible, not just topics or certain stories. You must not limit your education to word group studies or certain books as I talked about earlier. It is difficult to explain some topics without touching on others. Rabbit trails are often the case when teaching from scripture, for if one teaches the entire topic and all that ties to it, one would have to teach the entire Bible each time to teach a single lesson. Therefore, it is understandable why many students and teachers do not explore the entirety of any given subject. Instead, they learn enough about accompanying subjects to get their point across to help others along on the main subject. That is what we will be doing here, touching on a few topics (rabbit trails) to clarify my main point. It is not smart to pull any single scripture, or even small sections of scripture, out of its context. That will get you partial imagery, which in turn will lead one to an interpretation that our carnal, physical mind understands. The problem with that is that our mind receives 100 percent of its information from five natural, physical, carnal senses, and those conclusions—in most cases—will not line up with what a Spiritual God is trying to teach us. As I use scriptures, I encourage you to study long before each reference and long after to gain a fuller understanding of the imagery. I actually encourage you to read your Bible through a couple of times each year—or more—if you have time (if you do not have time, then make time, like throwing your TV away). By doing this, you steadily receive a transfer of the total image of what the Bible is saying from God's mind to yours.

Sadly, the mindset of today's microwave, impatient, generation is "entertain" me and do it quickly. Many more Christians that are more devoted read three-chapters-per-day in addition to studying someone else's notes on any given subject. This "three-chapters-per-day" is not bad, but it certainly is not God's best. He has prepared a table for you full of spiritual food- **Thou preparest a table before me in the presence of mine enemies: thou anointest my head with oil; my cup runneth over (Psalms 23:5).** That verse alone is a lesson in imagery. It is not talking about a wooden table loaded with perishable food. Rather, it is metaphor for imbibing or partaking of the spiritual knowledge, or "food", from the Bible. Think of the Bible lying flat, with four legs supporting it off the floor as if it were a table. It is loaded with a plethora of knowledge of how to live at peace, be healthy both physically and mentally, how to beat depression, have happy marriages, get off drugs, leave your past in the past, see through the lies of politics and so on. It is a genuine spiritual feast of all the spiritual knowledge of a relationship with Him that we need. He is just waiting for us to pull up a chair and eat our fill. God wants us to consume His word as if were spiritual food and sustenance, for it is in the unseen spiritual realm. Moreover, He has prepared it for you. So, go eat! There is not a thing the devil-the enemy- can do about it. We know he himself, cannot do anything about it. However, he can and will use his servants (our fellow humans) to stop us from getting our hands on the Bible. He hates that book with all his passion; he has tried to wipe the Bible from the earth, but has never been successful. Yet, his fools are still busy trying today.

We need the full image because partial imagery can lead one astray. Partial imagery ends in all kinds of wrong, misguided, and incomplete doctrines that make it unfruitful. In Psalms 1:3 and Jer. 17:8, God compares us to trees. Humans are not trees, so we know this is an analogy, or "imagery", of a deeper truth. A tree is known by its fruit, but if our doctrine is fruitless, i. e. does not accomplish any change in us, then we simply stay busy and are fruitless. To make that tree analogy more complicated to our carnal minds, the fruit He is looking for must be spiritual fruit, not *just* good works. Good works do produce good things, which are good for our fellow man, and in doing so makes us *feel* good about ourselves. However, it produces nothing in the spirit realm where God dwells. A quick example of this is to keep a "Sabbath" day. Some denominations keep Saturday, most keep Sunday. They sit in judgment of each other thinking that they are the one pleasing God. However, the Bible says- **One man esteemeth one day above another: another esteemeth every day *alike*. Let every man be fully persuaded in his own mind (Romans 14:5).** In short, God does not care what day you keep. You can keep either Saturday or Sunday, or no day at all. It does not affect your spiritual condition because the keeping of either day will not produce the spiritual fruit He is looking for. It can make you feel good that you did it, both emotionally and physically, but it has nothing to do with spiritual growth.

We see the zealous acts carried out by extremely zealous people (*much more devoted people than your average Christian*) who get a partial

How God Got Mary Pregnant

understanding of how much of a spiritual hindrance our fleshly bodies are to walking in the spirit- **And, the LORD said my spirit shall not always strive with man, for that he also *is* flesh… (Genesis 6:3).** Note the word "also". After the fall of man, all men (and women) by default, began to lose the knowledge of the fact that we were created to be more than just flesh. This means we lost our spiritual stride with God. Some zealots, who come to understand how our flesh gets in the way of the spirit will stop at that point, with that smaller revelation or knowledge, not the "full" revelation. It is a good day when any of us grow in grace and knowledge and come to understand that God really wants flesh out of the way. However, the process of separation will kill us, literally. Therefore, we have to stay in our flesh until death "doth part" our filthy flesh from our spirits, but we must live with the frustration of suppressing the flesh for the rest of our days on earth. We must place our flesh on the altar and take up that cross (to die on it) daily. These zealots I am referring to did not go on to consume enough of the Bible or get help from the Holy Spirit to get more revelation about how to suppress the flesh, but rather proceed to go on to act on that partial knowledge. This mistake is common to all of us that reach for and search for spiritual understanding. In our zeal (*bless our hearts*) and our human (*call it youthful*) ignorance and impatience, we run out ahead of our understanding and our carnal minds do not make the same choices a spirit-lead mind would. Even great men in the Lord have done that very thing. Two Hall-of-Famers, Moses and Abraham, are great examples of that very point. Moses knew he had a call on his life to free the Israelite's from Egypt. He took that partial knowledge and ran with it, which led him to murder a man. Abram had been told by God that he and Sarah would have a son, however, when it didn't happen as quickly as they thought it needed to, Abram, at Sarah's encouragement, took it upon himself to produce the offspring with another woman (Hagar) to get his God-given vision of an heir. However, all he started was earth's longest war between his two sons, Ishmael and Isaac. These two men had more excuse than do we because they could not be born again for Jesus had not yet made a way for that to happen in their time. Once we become born again, often—most often— our natural non-spiritual minds decide we want to do good works, good deeds, and good things, for a spiritual God. To proceed with partial truth and a partial image which the devil can steal easier than the complete image, we stray in our actions, which end in a spiritually fruitless endeavor. We see in the parable of the "sower", Mark 4:13-20, with focus on verse 15, that the devil comes to steal the word and he shows up to start preaching his twist on the truth we discovered- **And these are they** (*spiritually young zealous believers*) **by the way side, where the word is sown; but when they have heard, Satan cometh immediately, and taketh away the word that was sown in their hearts (Mark 4:15).**

In telling many lies, satan is hoping that one will become embedded in a zealot and take hold long enough to mislead us and others. Having lied to us, satan or best said his demons, observes us to see if we are going in the direction he has pointed us. Then he will hone that particular lie. The particular lie I am referring to with these zealots is when sincere people come to believe they must whip themselves with barbed wire, carry a cross on their knees on broken glass, put sharp rocks in their shoes (or other forms of painful submission), all in order to "punish" the flesh. The observer who does not understand the "wherefore and the why" will quickly draw the conclusion that these people are crazy. They are not crazy, but their actions do not draw many to Jesus, so the devil laughs himself silly at the misguided zeal because he knows it is a distraction from the real suppression of the flesh and will do nothing to win converts, it has just the opposite effect it turns potential converts away. Paul says- **"I therefore so run, not as uncertainly; so fight I, not as one that beateth the air" (I Cor. 9:26).** In modern terms, we would say they are "shadow boxing". There is place for the subjugation of our flesh, but barbed wire is not the answer. Paul goes on to say- **"But I keep under my body, and bring *it* into subjection: lest that by any means, when I have preached to others, I myself should be a castaway" (I Cor. 9:27).** In contrast to properly making the flesh submit, Paul talks about others who give complete control of their lives over to the flesh- **For many walk, of whom I have told you often, and now tell you even weeping, *that they are* the enemies of the cross of Christ: Whose end *is* destruction, whose God *is their* belly, and *whose* glory *is* in their shame, who mind earthly things (Philippians 3:18-19).**

The Bible has much to teach on the way flesh separates and blocks real spiritual life. Some examples of this would be: 1) The veil Moses wore to hide his shining face from the Israelite's; 2) The 4-inch thick veil that separated the inner court from the Holy of Holies in the temple that ripped the day Jesus died; 3) The fact that flesh was always put on the altar under the old covenant law, and; 4) The hymen in girls and the foreskin on boys, and the circumcision of it. Therefore, the zeal to do something about flesh is correct. To do it purposefully can bear much fruit; damaging the flesh will not. Jesus Himself told us- **"It is the spirit that quickeneth** (makes you spiritually alive)**; the flesh profiteth nothing: the words** (spiritual food) **that I speak unto you, *they* are spirit, and *they* are life"** (**John 6:63**)**.** What I mean is, to punish the house you live in will not change the "you" that lives in the house. To give too much, or the wrong, attention to the house (i. e. to damage or pamper it) does not bring spiritual life to the real you that lives inside of the flesh house. If your soul or mind is full of darkness (un-Godliness) due to ignorance of or past rejection of what is right, let in the light (the words of His book and the Divine helper—the Holy Ghost) and the darkness will be annihilated. Barbed wire and broken glass gets your mind on the pain but the gain is in your soul (such as extreme discipline), but not in your spirit. That is but one small example of partial imagery doing what partial imagery can do so easily—lead us astray.

The whole point of this imagery talk is to help you understand that if you, *your name here*_____do not consume the scriptures enough, then you have no idea if they, *nor I,* (or, whomever it may be) are lying to you or not. Moreover, your eternal salvation could be riding on this! Someone can tell you things that have you serving him or her and his or her dream or his or her organization, not God (hello religion). Here are some examples of these teachings: not wearing pants or jewelry, not eating certain foods or drinks, not marrying a divorced person— or not marrying at all, whether or not to drive a car— or only a certain color car, what day you attend church— or whether you are at church each time the doors are open, and the biggest lie of all *tithing*. The list can be nearly endless, I will make a point about tithing and get on with the main content of the book. This book is not mean to be a rant against religion, I can get on that soap box real quick in case you had not noticed already. But I do want to say something about tithing ...If your preacher teaches tithing there is only two categories they fit into.#1) They are ignorant of what the Bible actually teaches and should not be at the pulpit. Or#2) They do know what the Bible teaches and are liars, and should not be at the pulpit.

Many things taught by religion are only distractions from relationship with God. That is a devastating part of religion, for religion can keep you busy 70 years but you never get to know God. You do not want Him to say on judgment day, "I never knew you" (Matthew 7:22-23). I care about you as a fellow human walking through this messed up earth with me on a plight that we did not choose and we did not cause. I do not care for religion, although it is not all bad and it has a place. We see that example in humanity before the flood of Noah's day, and also with the nation of Israel after the flood. Before the flood, there was no law nor religion, which meant no book written as a guide, no moral code or fear of hell. The result of that was that the world got so wicked God had to wipe them off the earth and narrow mankind back down to eight people. Then the whole world, all eight of them, had knowledge of Him once more. After the flood, He began working a covenant, which was the only God-sanctioned religion ever to be on earth, which was the Law of Moses, given to the Israelite's. Today, He is drawing us towards something bigger and better; relationship, not duty. You do not need religion (because it normally consists of much duty that does not produce spiritual growth), you need Him, and He is all-good, all the time. Therefore, I encourage everyone to pray, and fast, and ask for the help of the Holy Spirit, and pour the Bible into you—it has the words of life. You will get the bigger picture, or *bigger image* I should say, of what God is doing here.

Keep in mind the people who wrote the Bible was doing so by the inspiration of God. It is a Holy Bible, not just a bible. It conveys the mind, the thoughts, the ways, and plans of a Holy God. It is not just the philosophy of men, or a group of philosophical thinkers who built on writings of others from earlier generations. The God who inspired the writing of the Bible lives in a spiritual realm where there is no death, decay, old age, thorns, sickness, or things that bite. He wanted us to be above what we are. He created us to operate in that spiritual world and this one (i. e. dual citizenship). He made this physical realm a mirror image of that spiritual realm, only without things that die, age, decay, thorns, sickness, or things that bite. Originally, He set this physical realm up to separate from that spiritual realm by the trigger of sin, when Adam would make that choice. God, in His wise foresight, designed our soul to dominate when the spirit-man failed to remain alive. Therefore when Adam rebelled, the dead, satanic-spirit he would receive would struggle to override the soul. Also at that moment, what we today call the second law of thermodynamics, is what sin introduced into the domain of men. I am not a scientist and if you want a detailed version of what the second law of thermodynamics is, go elsewhere to find it. A short, simple, explanation is: that things go from a higher state of order to a lower state of disorder. All things seek out the lowest state of equilibrium. An example of this is simple heat and cold. No matter what we do to contain heat, cold disperses it, and the cold will win in the end. The source of energy disperses that energy until it is no longer energetic, and cold wins the struggle, cruel entropy rules in the end. Young folks have more energy and generally better health than old folks do, but in time (which did not affect us before sin), they spend their energy and in the end .God simply calls it "death". He told Adam after he sinned- **In the sweat of thy face shalt thou eat bread, till thou return unto the ground; for out of it wast thou taken: for dust thou *art,* and unto dust shalt thou return (Gen. 3:19).** God made the universe alive; Adam chose via sin to kill it. God created the universe to be in a constant state of rejuvenation, not a state of decay. However, sin happened and the universe became just like the bad tree Adam had eaten from, and now his domain is ruled spiritually by darkness and death, which is of satan, who introduced all the things we do not like about this world. God saw all this unfold *before* it did and told us all the details we needed to make the right choice. Therefore, to call the Bible "God's word" and "Holy," which it rightfully is, we must understand it is not simply the words or writings of people. The book is too fascinating to come from human origins (that alone would require a large book to explain). *For further understanding of this rabbit trail, study "apologetics".*

There are many good books out about the Bible, but you must be careful what you read, for sadly, many books just teach to itching ears what the institution of religion needs for you to continue hearing for their best interest. How can you know? The answer is by telling God you want the Holy Spirit's help (read John chapter 14-15), which you need because the Bible is a spiritual book written from a spiritual point of view. By default, we being carnal and physical from birth, our minds think carnally and physically, and will by default draw wrong conclusions about what the Bible is saying. Then after you have asked the Holy Ghost for His help, go read the Bible over and over and over, again and again and again. By doing so, you are pouring spiritual food into your spiritual mind and physical mind (soul). The Helper you asked God for—the Holy Ghost—will begin to give your physical mind an understanding of what you are reading, and it will gradually become clearer to your soul. You will have a steady transformation from carnal thinking to spiritual thinking. That way you will know when another book does not line up with scripture. You will begin to know when incorrect doctrine, carved out (engraved) by the tongues of physical-minded religious brokers, violates the image building inside of you. God says to not "make any graven images", but that is what much of religion does. Religion will have you worshiping a Jesus that only remotely resembles the real Jesus. Such as: and to my knowledge this is the biggest misconception of Jesus out there in religion and that is: That He was fully God and fully man. That He was Deity while He was on this earth. THAT IS NOT TRUE. I'll get on that soap box a few minutes. So many Christians out there believe that Jesus remained Deity while He was on earth. If He were Deity the pleasures of sin would have meant nothing to Him, meaning they would not tempt Him in any way. Note the last part of this verse…..**Let no man say when he is tempted, I am tempted of God: for God cannot be tempted with evil, neither tempteth he any man:** If God cannot be tempted with evil then Jesus could not have been Deity/God while living in a flesh body for Jesus was tempted, what we see next is basically Jesus being told by the referee to put your mouth-guard in, your gloves on and climb into the boxing ring... **(Jas 1:13) Then was Jesus led up of the Spirit into the wilderness to be tempted of the devil. (Mat 4:1)** Jesus was going out there into the dessert to face off with satan the same way Adam did and lost humanity. Jesus was going out there as a man JUST LIKE ADAM WAS to face our adversary in the exact same way, the prize again was humanity. If it was Deity fighting satan there was not struggle, no fight at all, satan would not have even shown up to

How God Got Mary Pregnant

get into the ring. But he had a chance to win because he knew he was up against a mortal man, same as he had been 4000 years earlier with Adam. Adam was God's mortal son alive with a spirit that came from God. Jesus was God's mortal son alive with a spirit that came from God. In his mind satan had this so he showed up. I want you to get this, you as a student must take steps to ensure you are following after truth so in addition to reading, pray equally as much as you read the Word, and fast as often as you can to put your flesh in its proper place (under your spirit and soul). All of these things will aid in this transformation of making your flesh bow to your spirit. Now, here are A few words on fasting, then I will finish this thought…

Fasting

When I was about 12-14 years old, I did an "accidental experiment" with a puppy I had. I was just goofing off at the time. What I learned fits well as a teaching tool for this topic of fasting, and I wanted to share it so that you could get an image of what happens inside you when we start trying to suppress our flesh to exalt our spirit. I had raised this dog from a pup. I had petted it, wrestled with it, and spoiled it. It loved me and I loved it. One day, when he was about 6-8 months old, he was playing in an empty room. Looking in, I got the idea that it would be interesting to see what he did if I came in with a ski mask on, arms raised high, wailing and growling loudly. I did all that and kept steadily walking toward the pup. The reaction from the "beast" ties interestingly in with how our flesh reacts when fasting. My puppy reacted in confusion at first and began to back away from me. It backed itself into a corner. When it became aware that it was cornered, it went into self-preservation mode and turned on me— showing its teeth, growling, and raising the hair on his back. He would have charged me had I not ended my terrorizing tactics. If you chance to do this with your dog, you can end this experiment quickly by pulling the mask off and speaking softly to it in your normal voice. Use good judgment, if your dog is mean as sin or as big as a calf then maybe it would not be wise.

Jeremiah C. Southerman

You need to run the following experiment on yourself. This will give you insight into what I am teaching, and a glimpse into the difference between spirit, soul, and body. If you have not done the Romans 10:9-10 thing, then you need to do that now, for this will not make much sense to you if you still have a dead spirit housed inside your flesh body. I will do my best to explain either way. Here goes: If you want to "see" your flesh and better understand the three-in-one nature of how God made you, then this will show you the one-third of you that is flesh (i. e. the "beast" in you). To make this successful you need at least a three or four day fast, it may not work on a fast as short as that, if not, go seven or ten days. If you are freaking out right now at the thought of fasting one day then you will have to work your way up to a three-day fast. It is *not* hard on your body, it is your mind/soul, i. e. a mindset that needs changed, for right now your body dictates to your mind, "feed me"!, (Your body is in charge). Fasting a few days at time will get your mind in the mindset that *it,* not your flesh, is in charge. (*Moves you towards "stage two", more on that later.*) I say try a one day fast and see what happens. If you have no negative "reactions" (I doubt you will with only one day), then keep your fast going. Please note that if you have diabetes or other serious health issues, then this approach needs modification and may need the approval of your doctor. What you will see is this: Your flesh, being used to being petted and stroked, love and pampering all of its life will react a lot like my puppy. You love your flesh and you think it loves you; it is your "pet". However, fasting will put the "mask" on your soul. Your flesh will not understand what your soul is doing to it and after about three days, it will go into self-preservation mode and turn on you. Your emotions will get raw and you can be mad at anything and everything all at once, for no apparent reason. It takes dedication of your soul to make this work, for in most cases, if you have not done the Romans 10:9-10 thing, then your soul has no help from a Godly, re-born spirit. Because your dead-spirit is not alive to support your soul in suppressing the flesh, your soul will side with your pet flesh. But, hopefully, those who are born-again, with living spirits, will see how calm and joyous your spirit is while your flesh thinks it is going to die; and your soul will walk away with an education. The experiment will yield education, understanding, and vision of this three-in-oneness of us, and where there is no knowledge, God's people perish- **Where *there is***

How God Got Mary Pregnant

no vision, the people perish: but he that keepeth the law, happy *is* he (Proverbs 29:18).

Now back to my thought before the topic of fasting interrupted it. There will be many parts of books, other than the Bible, that are good for sound doctrine. On the other hand, some doctrinal ideas in those same books need discarded as rubbish. The Holy Spirit, coupled with the knowledge you have been pouring into your soul from the Bible, will confirm the validity of what the books are saying. Now we will look at God's three-in-oneness.

GOD IS: 1

Jehovah, the Father

We will start with the oldest point of reference there is and that would be before there was time. Our brains work best in time, so... 300 trillion years ago, let's say (*just for a reference number*), God was,#1) Jehovah,#2) Word, and#3) Holy Spirit. His main attribute is love (I John 4:8 and I John 4:16) and that in His love He had a plan and in that plan He included you. Yes, I said you! *Your name here again, please*_____.
God wants you to be with Him where He is and to be like Him and live forever with His family. However, an obstacle got in the way. Actually two obstacles did. One was lucifer, and the other was your grandpa. Not the grandpa you have photos of or know personally, but one about 200 generations back (*give or take a few*); his name was Adam. There were interesting things happening before Adam was here, so let us look at those to see the first obstacle.

Job was a man that lived not long after the flood of Noah's day. We get a glimpse of "time" in the book of Job. God is asking Job a question- **Where wast thou** (*Job*) **when I** (*God*) **laid the foundations of the earth? Declare, if thou hast understanding. Who hath laid the measures thereof, if thou knowest? Or who hath stretched the line upon it? Whereupon are the foundations thereof fastened? Or who laid the corner stone thereof; When the morning stars** (*probably angels*) **sang together and all the sons** (*angels*) **of God shouted for joy? (Job 38:4-7).**

If you are a "Sci-fi" fan, you may get what I am about to talk about easily, which is higher dimensional stuff (*there is only four pages of it*) since science fiction writers often use higher dimensions in their books. If you do not know what "sci-fi" is, then you are *not* a fan, it does not matter. What I am about to teach helps our small limited minds to frame up a God that is bigger than our mind can conceive; not that He will fit into any frame our mind can dream up, but this helps. This explanation is not based on the science and the math that people like Stephen Hawking and Michio Kaku handle (*in fact, this isn't based on any math at all*). I do find it interesting that "M-Theory", the most advanced Grand Unified Theories (GUT, in physics terms) requires 11 dimensions. And like my theory here to follow, there is really no way to measure any of this higher dimensional stuff in our 4-dimensional labs, we have to gain this knowledge of the invisible (to us) by observing what is visible. Sounds like- **For the invisible things of him from the creation of the world are clearly seen, being understood by the things that are made,** *even* **his eternal power and Godhead; so that they are without excuse (Romans 1:20).** This is a simple example of imagery from the Bible. I had zero help from the people smarter and more educated than me to come up with this; it is straight from the Bible to my soul. It is simple, I just pray I can explain it well. Here goes:

We take up three dimensions of space. We have height (how tall we are), width (how wide we are), and depth (how thick we are from front to rear). We know that God created all things. Angels, like us, are things (i. e. beings that needed a starting point). In addition, these angels occupy dimensions of space relative to each other, and that realm is above our abilities. He gives us guidelines we *can* relate to in the Bible. For example, when we read of angels appearing and interacting with humans, we see that they did so in a 3-dimensional human-like form. This is not their natural

Jeremiah C. Southerman

form, but we as humans, have no idea what that natural form is. I am going to assume that in their natural form, they take up all dimensions of space in their realm, or maybe it will help to say they "fill-up" their personal space. Picture them walking up to each other and speaking. They would have height, width, and depth relative to each other. It may not be as we (in our 3-dimensional abilities) would see them, but they would be similar or equal to the way we would see each other. From their point of view there would be no empty voids around them (as in, we fill-up our space), which is a normal and natural point of view for them, just as 3 dimensions are normal and natural for us. That may not sound very clear to some, so let me try it again. In their realm they take up space. Just as two of us cannot occupy the same space at the same time, neither can they, for they occupy a space with their bodies. The space they would occupy would be height, width, and depth, plus a-b-c. They are higher dimensional beings than we are, so I suppose they take up six dimensions, but our minds cannot think in six, so picture them in three as they greet each other. In addition, picture God in 3-D, for it helps our small minds. God said He sits on a throne; His throne occupies three dimensions of space in a realm far above our imagination. Again, He uses 3-D terminology that is similar to things in our world so that we can better picture His domain without it "scrambling" our minds. Therefore, it is not an insult to Him if we think of His throne as an elevated chair (a grand one) and it takes up space as a chair does in our realm. God describes Himself as having arms, hands, eyes, feet, nostrils. In short, He made us to look like Him. With that information, it is a safe assumption that He looks like us. When He manifests Himself to a lower dimensional creature, He does so in a fashion that the lower creature can understand Him, just as angels do with us. If God looks like us then He takes up three space-dimensions as well that our minds can frame Him in. He has height, width and depth, plus a-b-c-x-y and z, which our minds cannot frame Him into. With this idea, let us go forward in time. At one point, before time in any dimension, there was only God sitting in His 11th 10th and 9th dimensions, which is the third heaven. Then He caused a change—He created angels that will not die and with them came a time that would not end. This would be the 7th, 6th, and 5th space-dimensions. Moreover, they have their own time, which we will number as the 8th dimension. This is the 2nd heaven, and all these are above ours. That time, where the angelic realm dwells, is not counted by clocks on walls as our time is. Then later, there came a creation of our universe and a new time came along with it. This would be the 4-dimensional space-time continuum as we know it and can measure it. This would be the 3rd, 2nd, and 1st space dimensions and they sit in a time dimension of their own that Albert Einstein named the 4th dimension, and this makes up the 1st heaven. The 1st heaven sets above us but is the part of our dimension where we fly planes and rockets, but we ourselves cannot be there without mechanical help.

So, a quick recap, but this time we will count up, not down. We have humanity living in 3 space-dimensions and 1 of time; that is 4 dimensions, which contains the 1st heaven. Then we have the angelic creation. They have 3 space-dimensions known as their realm and 1 of time; this is the 2nd heaven. The angels can manifest and function in our three dimensions so that is six of space for them, plus their own time. The total so far is eight, our time has no effect on angels so it is not relevant to them. Then, God lives in three space-dimensions of His own beyond the others and there is no time there, and this is the 3rd heaven.

Another way to recap:

Man- 1st, 2nd, 3rd dimensions of space, plus 1 of time=4 dimensions.
Angels- 5th, 6th, 7th, dimensions of space, plus 1 of their time=8 dimensions.
God- 9th, 10th and 11th dimensions of space, with no time=11 dimensions.

While there is no direct wording in the Bible to support a 1st and 2nd heaven, you cannot get to a 3rd without having a 1st and 2nd (*this is imagery at work)*. Paul talks about his visit to the 3rd heaven in, II Cor. 12:2- **I knew a man in Christ above fourteen years ago, (whether in the body, I cannot tell; or whether out of the body, I cannot tell: God knoweth) such an one caught up to the third heaven.** We see references to the word heavens (plural) 133 times in the Bible. Here are two that make the point clearly: 1) **Behold, the heaven and the heaven of heavens *is* the LORD'S thy God, the earth *also*, with all that therein *is*. (Deut. 10:14).** And, 2) **Praise him, ye heavens of heavens, and ye waters that *be* above the**

heavens (Psa. 148:4). This paints a good, clear image that there is more than one, so again, it is impossible to get to a 3rd without having 1st and 2nd.

We must seek God's fullness, we seek until we find, and we knock until the door is open to us. We must desire a relationship with Him before we can discover deeper things about Him. It is not that He holds back or hides from us, only that it takes above average diligence to push through our veil of flesh to get to where we can see Him. It cannot be a lack-luster desire, it must truly consume us. This desire must be almost like an addiction, such as alcohol to the alcoholic, without all the destruction that addiction brings, of course. In the discovery process, we continue finding new depths. Since satan never took time to get to know The Godhead, then satan never found out The Godhead was bigger than satan ever dreamed, bigger than the 8-dimensional space-time continuum the angelic world lives in. God would manifest Himself in the 2nd heaven and to the angels living in the 5th, 6th, and 7th dimensions. He seemed to be a complete being or person in their realm. I think His throne is a full and complete throne as it manifests in the lower eight dimensions as counted by the angels occupying the lower set of dimensions. It is my belief that the angels do not have access to the highest dimensions where His fullness is experienced. I believe that special experience is reserved for family; the family that has been denied God for 6000 years and counting. This family is the born-again believers with oil in their lamps that endure until the end. I do not mean to limit God to eleven dimensions, ultimately, so maybe the family arena is the 12th dimension and maybe there are hundreds more... maybe even a trillion, but I am going to stay with eleven for now.

To get that family, God made us like Him. But we are not Deity, will never be Deity, not even when all is said and done and we have all received our glorified bodies will we be Deity. However, we will then be fully manifested family members in close personal contact with Him in glory. To be with Him in His highest levels He had to make us in His image, in His likeness, which is higher than the angels are. To understand this better, we will look at ourselves as a reference since we know what humans look like- **And God said, Let us make man in our image, after our likeness: and let them have dominion over the fish of the sea, and over the fowl**

How God Got Mary Pregnant

of the air, and over the cattle, and over all the earth, and over every creeping thing that crept upon the earth (Gen. 1:26).

"Us" is a plural term meaning more than one person of the Godhead. There is God Jehovah (I often think of Him as the "throne sitter" who oversees all things). He is the one who would later become the Father God of Jesus the Son. At this particular time, another Person of the Godhead was "The Word": His name is "The Word." Think of Him as a spokesperson, or voice, of God. The Word would later become human, enter into His creation, and buy us back from satan by paying the ransom price set on us because of sin. The other person of the Godhead is the Holy Spirit, or often called, the Holy Ghost. He is the one that does the works of God. He has no single body. He is everywhere at once and He can manifest Himself as many times as needed simultaneously without diminishing any of Himself in anyway (He is omnipresent). They are all one. For you to whom this is new, this brings new meaning to the saying, "me, myself and I". Here is the way we see them work: Jehovah decides what they are going to do, the Word speaks it, and the Holy Spirit makes it happen. This is the "us" when it says, "let *us* make man in our image". All three *"parts"* (for lack of a better word) comprise the whole Deity. Since God made us in His image and in His likeness, we also have a spirit, soul and body, with all three working together to compose the whole human. We can, therefore reckon, and God will not be angry if we miss it, that He has a soul and a body, and we *"know"* He is a Spirit. This may help: To explore how we are three-in-one adds to our understanding of Him. Our spirit can influence our soul to do a good deed if our spirit is being lead by God. Alternatively, if our spirit is still being lead by the devil, it can influence us to engage in a selfish act. The spirit is part one of us. Our soul, or mind—which is part two of us—chooses which way to go, then instructs our body—part three—to carry out whether we are going to help the old lady across the street or try to steal her purse.

I think God literally has a soul and He lives in a spirit body. Think of the body that God has as "invisible-matter" (that is, invisible to a 3-dimensional human and a 6-dimensional angel). Whether that is correct or not is beyond our knowing at this time, but it helps our small minds grasp something.

25

Astronomers today know that dark energy (invisible and un-measurable to us at this time) is driving the expansion of our universe, (at least that is the mainstream theory call it "doctrine" right now. The James Webb telescope is changing our view and we will have to modify our educational approach with what we are learning from it.) So the concept of invisible forces at work is not that strange. The "invisible substance" that God seems to use in His highest realm (such as the throne He sits on) would be similar to, but higher than, what He made angels out of, for they are invisible to us as well. Another way I can think to relay what I mean is that our eyes and brain can only see into, and conceive of, 3 space- dimensions, so it's not that this matter is really invisible, just outside of our range of perception, much like infrared and ultraviolet light is. Angels are invisible to us until they choose to manifest themselves in our lower dimension. God, being higher than the angels, would be invisible to them until He chose to manifest Himself to them in their lower dimension. They would see Him as complete and total being, unaware by observation or any kind of laboratory test, that He was anything more than they could touch with their 6-dimensional senses. These following verses refer to God and tell us what He is like. In these verses, I have put the word "soul" in italics.

God has a soul: First "part"

Isaiah 1:14- Your new moons and your appointed feasts my... *soul...***hateth: they are a trouble unto me; I am weary to bear them.**

Jeremiah 5:29- Shall I not visit for these *things?* **saith the LORD: shall not my...***soul***...be avenged on such a nation as this?**

Matt. 12:18- Behold my servant, whom I have chosen; my beloved, in whom my...*soul***...is well pleased: I will put my spirit upon him, and he shall shew judgment to the Gentiles.**

Hebrews 10:38- Now the just shall live by faith: but if any man draw back, my...*soul***...shall have no pleasure in him.** Clearly, God has a soul. Next, let's discuss His body.

God has a body: Second "part"

He talks many times about "His arm", such as in, Isa. 51:9, 53:1, and John 12:38. Also, He speaks of the "earth as His footstool" in Ps. 99:5, 110:1, 132:7, Isa. 66:1 Matt 5:35, and Matt 22:44. Then "His hand" is referred to in Ex. 9:3, 16:3, Duet. 2:15, and Ps 118:1. He describes his eyes in Gen. 6:8, Deut 13:18, 1st Sam 26:24, 1st King 8:29& 52, 1st King 11:33, 5:15,& 11, 1st Kings 16:25, Zech. 4:10 and 1st Peter 3:12. These are just a few scriptural references for each. Ezekiel saw Him on what seems to be His portable throne (Ezekiel chapter 1), and His "legs" looked like brass and His "hair" like fire. God uses wool and many other things to describe Himself. Many times the Bible touches on His "body". The book of Revelation talks about the eyes of the glorified Jesus (as He looks today), and likens them to "fire". While on earth, Jesus said- **Have I been so long time with you, and yet hast thou not known me, Philip? he that hath seen me hath seen the Father; and how sayest thou _then,_ Shew us the Father? (John 14:9).** I believe one, but not all the reasons Jesus said this was to show that God made us to look like Himself, having two eyes and two ears, a nose, a bi-ped with two arms, and so on. Therefore, I think it is safe to conclude that God has a body. Next, let us look at what He tells us the most about Himself.

God is a Spirit: Third "part"

The next thing we will look at is the fact that He is a Spirit. This is the primary attribute referred to in the Bible- **God is a Spirit: and they that worship him must worship him in spirit and in truth (John 4:24).** He also says- **Furthermore, we have had fathers of our flesh which corrected _us,_ and we gave _them_ reverence: shall we not much rather be in subjection unto the Father of spirits, and live (Hebrews 12:9).** Pretty much all I can say concerning the spirit (_I am too carnal- minded to do otherwise_) is that it is higher than we know. Humans tend to look up towards heaven when we pray, acknowledging that He is above us, and I think that is more metaphoric than an actual place He resides. Outer space is "up" or "above" us relative to our point of view from the surface of the

Jeremiah C. Southerman

earth. To a penguin living on an iceberg at the North Pole, his "down" is an "up" direction relative to a penguin at the South Pole. "Up above us" or "higher than us" is not actually a direction that God is from us. It is more a concept in our minds. The best little book I know on this concept written in 1884 called <u>Flatland: A Romance of Many Dimensions,</u> or, "<u>Flatland</u>," for short, by Edwin A. Abbott. It will help one understand how things could, or may work, in a spiritual, "higher" realm relative to our abilities. The "Spirit" realm of God is higher than the angel's realm, even though they are made of spirit. Therefore, with these verses, it gives us a better image of who we are (the three-in-one way He created us) and how it relates to what God is like.

GOD IS: 2

The Holy Ghost
(Also known as the Holy Spirit)

We often interchange the name Holy Ghost or Holy Spirit because they mean the same thing. The Holy Spirit is the member of the Godhead that is the power behind the works done first by Jesus, then Jesus' followers. An example of this would be that Jesus did no miracle until after He was baptized and the Holy Spirit came down on Him in the form of a dove- **John bare record, saying, I saw the Spirit descending from heaven like a dove, and it abode upon him (John 1:32).** I know there are *so called* Bible teachers out there that teach Jesus did miracles all His life as a young boy, like healing birds wings and other things prior to the wedding and turning water into wine, but the Bible plainly says…… **This beginning of miracles did Jesus in Cana of Galilee, and manifested forth his glory; and his disciples believed on him. (John 2:11)** Also see Matt. 3:16, Mark 1:10 and Luke 3:22. We see the Holy Spirit come into the upper room "like a mighty rushing wind", and they (120 people) were filled with The Holy Spirit (see Acts chapter 2). Then the 120 spoke with new tongues (120 different languages that they never learned) to the masses in the streets in Jerusalem. In addition, they spoke with a boldness as they preached the gospel. The boldness to preach the gospel came from an understanding of it revealed to them by the indwelling of this same Holy Spirit, who clarified the scriptures they had been consuming and the teaching Jesus had given them. Jesus said- **And I** (Jesus) **will pray the Father, and he shall give you** (believers that follow Me) **another Comforter, that he** (the Holy Spirit) **may abide with you forever;** *Even* **the Spirit of truth; whom the world cannot receive,** (because He will not indwell or abide with a dead spirit for it would annihilate the spiritually dead person before they had a change of spirit) **because it** (the world and the dead spiritual/carnal beings in it) **seeth him not, neither knoweth him: but ye know him; for he dwelleth with you, and shall be in you (John 14:16-17).** And He will never leave us or forsake us, but we can leave Him if we are not content with Him- *Let your* **conversation** *be* **without covetousness;** *and be* **content with such things as ye have: for he hath said, I will never leave thee, nor forsake thee. So that we may boldly say, The Lord** *is* **my helper, and I will not fear what man shall do unto me (Hebrews 13:5-6).**

GOD IS: 3

The Word, who became Jesus

Now let us get to the third person of the Godhead. This Word "character" is Mary's little boy. "The Word" is also the Word of God as a book, …Ah, that would be the "Holy Bible", in particular for our day, the King James version, since it is the best we have to work with today. The King James Bible, written in the year 1611, in 400+ year old English, can be a slight challenge to read since it is not so common today. However, it is still not even that hard for modern readers to understand. When satan tells your spirit-man that lie (*that it is old English and too hard to read*) he watches to see if you are in his mindset, and when you agree with him and say, "I cannot understand all the "thees" and "thous", so I'm not going to read it. I am speaking from experience, and can tell you once you begin consuming the King James it will flow into your soul just fine. I am not one of those people that religiously say you *must* use the King James. It is flowery, poetic, and at times, a little cumbersome. I have found that it is the best baseline to build doctrine on, however. I also like the amplified version as a good read but I would not advise building doctrine on it. There is a

Jeremiah C. Southerman

version called the <u>New King James</u> where they did not try to re-translate it, just brought the English up to date. Therefore, if thouest findeth it troublesome to readest thus, thou shalt get the New King James and you will find it less cumbersome. Now, on to this "Word" fellow.

JOHN 1:1-14

We will go to some scripture and look at what Mary agreed to when she said in Luke 1:38, "be it unto me". Beginning in John 1:1 through verse 14. We will read these verses once before we revisit them. Then I will attempt to build and clarify the image the second time through the verses; the imagery is not really an abstract image to get, but to break it down does help if you have not meditated on it for months. Sometimes an image takes years of meditation to receive clearly but this one is not that hard.

John 1:1-In the beginning was the Word, and the Word was with God, and the Word was God. John 1:2-The same was in the beginning with God. John 1:3-All things were made by him; and without him was not anything made that was made. John 1:4-In him was life; and the life was the light of men. John 1:5-And the light shineth in darkness; and the darkness comprehended it not. John 1:6-There was a man sent from God, whose name *was* John. John 1:7-The same came for a witness, to bear witness of the Light, that all *men* through him might believe. John 1:8-He was not that Light, but *was sent* to bear witness of that Light. John 1:9-That was the true Light, which lighteth every man that cometh into the world. John 1:10-He was in the world, and the world was made by him, and the world knew him not. John

1:11-He came unto his own, and his own received him not. John 1:12- But as many as received him, to them gave he power to become the sons of God, *even* to them that believe on his name: John 1:13-Which were born, not of blood, nor of the will of the flesh, nor of the will of man, but of God. John 1:14-And the Word was made flesh, and dwelt among us, (and we beheld his glory, the glory as of the only begotten of the Father,) full of grace and truth.

Now let us break it down:

John 1:1-In the beginning... chronologically speaking, this is the oldest verse in the Bible. This begins before there was a beginning of time, as angels or we count it **was the Word, and the Word was with God, and the Word was God.** "Word" was His name back then. "Back then" is a relative term because before there was a creation, there was no time.

John 1:2-The same God Being named "The Word" **was in the beginning with God**, because He was one-third of the Godhead.

John 1:3- All things were made by him; this supernatural God Being called "The Word" **and without him** The Being called, "The Word", **was not anything made that was made.**

John 1:4- In him The God Being called "The Word" **was life;** real life, everlasting life, spiritual life **and the** spiritual **life was the** spiritual **light of men.**

John 1:5- And the spiritual **light** of the man within or inside of Jesus that came with Him out of Mary's womb **shineth in** the spiritual **darkness;** of the fallen kingdoms of men caused by Adam's rebellion and we are held in darkness by satan and sin **and the** spiritual **darkness** that we and our fallen darkened minds are so locked into **comprehended it not.** The "it" here refers to the spiritual light of Him, and the spiritual light that He walked in, we comprehended *it* not.

John 1:6- **There was a man sent from God, whose name *was* John.** This John is "John the Baptist" or John "the baptizer", not the apostle John who is writing this gospel.

John 1:7- **The same** John **came for a witness,** to speak words **to bear witness of the Light,** The Light was the spiritual light of the man Jesus, so **that all *men* through him** Jesus **might believe.**

John 1:8- **He** John, **was not that** spiritual **Light, but *was sent* to bear witness** verbally preach and teach others **of that** unseen long forgotten by humanity, that spiritual **light,** which would once again be on earth in Jesus.

John 1:9- ***That*** God Being called "The Word" that now came to humanity in a human form (i. e. flesh) **was the true Light, which lighteth every man that cometh into the world.**

John 1:10- **He** Jesus, the God Being formerly called, "The Word" of God **was in the world, and the world was made by him, and the world knew him not** because the world was spiritually dead and could not truly grasp anything spiritual in nature.

John 1:11- **He,** Jesus, the Being formerly called "The Word" **came unto his own,** This can be taken two ways, both are correct,#1) He came to humanity as one of us, (human) and humanity received Him not.#2) And, He came unto His own people; His own tribe of the Israelite's, Judah, **and his own** Jews **received him not.**

John 1:12- **But as many** Jew or gentile **as received him, to them gave he power to become the sons of God *even* to them that believe on his name:** This means younger brothers and sisters to Jesus Himself, which makes God our Father. That is because something happens in the invisible spiritual realm.

John 1:13- And that thing that happens is that they who believe **which were born, not of blood, nor of the will of the flesh, nor of the will of man, but of God.** who is a Spirit, is talking about being "born again" and that was the plan from the beginning. He would come to earth to be like Adam (His first created living being of the human race). He would face satan just as Adam did, defeat satan where Adam failed, and by doing so, would open up a door for us to the heavenly Spirit realm; the same door that Adam closed in his act of rebellion. Moreover, all we have to do is believe in Him to become a part of His kingdom. Look at it this way, Adam had more faith in the visible physical world that he could touch with his five senses than he did in God's words, which was Adam's ticket out of God's kingdom. Our ticket back into God's kingdom is to have more faith in the unseen spiritual realm in which God words—the Holy Bible—tells us about than the physical world around us that we can touch with our five senses.

John 1:14- And the Spirit Being called the **Word was made flesh,** left the Almighty power of His Deity behind in heaven, housed His pure spirit (small "s" that was just like the spirit He gave Adam) in a body that had been prepared for Him, then came to a virgin named Mary. Mary agreed to the plan and God deposited "the seed" in her womb. Nine months later, she gave birth to Word, The I Am, Jesus, Emanuel **and** The Word. Jesus, I Am, Emanuel, **dwelt among us, (and we beheld his glory, the glory as of the only begotten of the Father) full of grace and truth.** So now, we have one-third of the Godhead, now a human, housed in flesh, born as a baby to a virgin named Mary. Mary was married to a man named Joseph whom had not yet had sex with her, who was not Jesus' father. Now that we have discussed briefly who and what God is and what He is doing and why we are here, let's now go look at what got in the way of God's original plan.

THE OBSTACLES

Lucifer's Thinking; Evil Invented

In the angelic realm, God made three archangels higher than the rest of the angels to be leaders. Each would be over one-third of the angels (*which I think number in the trillions*). These three were Michael, Gabriel and lucifer. Because lucifer is so vain, he steals the spotlight, for now, from the other two. They are cool (at ease) with that, and they will remain cool (at ease) for eternity while he is hot, very hot, hot like the lake of fire is hot—actually, the same exact thermal reading, in fact. Let us go back 10 trillion years this time (*I seem to like that trillion number*). Back then, lucifer was the leader of the band, the music director, or the rock star. He was "music" and he wrote the songs; he was the choir leader in heaven's church service. That job he did well. We know that because God does what He does right and He created a music "man" full of the ability to make music and full of musical talent. We get another glimpse of lucifer in the book of Ezekiel. This section of the Bible, addressed to the "king of tyrus", who is only a man, but that man was like adolph hitler. In that tyrus was possessed by satan himself, so God was addressing the wicked spirit being, satan, inside

37

Jeremiah C. Southerman

the man tyrus. As one reads this, it is easy to see that this was not a mere mortal man- **Moreover the word of the LORD came unto me, saying, Son of man, take up a lamentation upon the king of Tyrus, and say unto him, Thus saith the Lord GOD; Thou sealest up the sum, full of wisdom, and perfect in beauty. Thou hast been in Eden the garden of God; every precious stone *was* thy covering, the sardius, topaz, and the diamond, the beryl, the onyx, and the jasper, the sapphire, the emerald, and the carbuncle, and gold: the workmanship of thy tabrets and of thy pipes was prepared in thee in the day that thou wast created. Thou *art* the anointed cherub that covereth; and I have set thee *so:* thou wast upon the holy mountain of God; thou hast walked up and down in the midst of the stones of fire. Thou *wast* perfect in thy ways from the day that thou wast created, till iniquity was found in thee. By the multitude of thy merchandise they have filled the midst of thee with violence, and thou hast sinned: therefore I will cast thee as profane out of the mountain of God: and I will destroy thee, O covering cherub, from the midst of the stones of fire. Thine heart was lifted up because of thy beauty, thou hast corrupted thy wisdom by reason of thy brightness: I will cast thee to the ground, I will lay thee before kings, that they may behold thee. Thou hast defiled thy sanctuaries by the multitude of thine iniquities, by the iniquity of thy traffick; therefore will I bring forth a fire from the midst of thee, it shall devour thee, and I will bring thee to ashes upon the earth in the sight of all them that behold thee. All they that know thee among the people shall be astonished at thee: thou shalt be a terror, and never *shalt* thou *be* any more (Ezekiel 28:11-19).**

We see that God created lucifer with the ability to make music with every part of his very body; he did not need musical instruments. This tells us that music sways emotions in the spirit world the same as it does in our physical world, which in turn can affect our moods and our thinking. Animals do not have this for God did not make them in His image. I am going to assume that angels have brains of some higher order and are like ours in similar ways. Based on that assumption we can conclude that when it was time for worship, lucifer would come out on the stage and the angelic host would be excited for they knew that when the mood was set,

How God Got Mary Pregnant

Jehovah would show up, and oh, was that good. During worship times, God would manifest Himself there with the angelic host in the 2nd heaven, which is the 5th, 6th, and 7th space dimension. He was in His fullness as far as they could figure since they could not ever see Him in His fullness because, just as we cannot see into higher dimensions, neither can they. They could walk up to Him, touch Him, and walk around Him because He had no strings or source of energy supporting Him from elsewhere. He was a complete and total being as far as they could understand. We see this in the New Testament when Jesus just appeared in the room after heaven received Him to be glorified, and had returned to earth for a forty day visitation back on earth- **And they rose up the same hour, and returned to Jerusalem, and found the eleven gathered together, and them that were with them, Saying, The Lord is risen indeed, and hath appeared to Simon. And they told what things *were done* in the way, and how he was known of them in breaking of bread. And as they thus spake, Jesus himself stood in the midst of them, and saith unto them, Peace *be* unto you. But they were terrified and affrighted, and supposed that they had seen a spirit. And he said unto them, Why are ye troubled? and why do thoughts arise in your hearts? Behold my hands and my feet, that it is I myself: handle me, and see; for a spirit hath not flesh and bones, as ye see me have (Luke 24:33-39).** He was real. They could walk up to Him, touch Him, talk to Him, walk completely around Him, drop a hula-hoop over His head, and it would drop to the floor. He could step out of the hula-hoop and play skip-a-rope with them. In every sense of the word, Jesus was fully there. He even told them to check him out, just after He appeared in the room (read Luke 24:39 again). As far as we four-dimensional creatures count fullness, Jesus was complete, self-contained, and in need of no kind of tie to a higher realm to power Him while He was in that room, in our four-dimensional space-time.

I think lucifer failed to realize he was locked into a smaller set of dimensions than God was. Lucifer thought too highly of himself. He understood the esteemed position that God had given him and he liked *it* more than he should. He knew that he was the one who got things going in the worship service and he made sure he did it well. He was so involved making sure he did his *duty* perfectly for the worship service, that he never

Jeremiah C. Southerman

got involved *in* the worship service. This failure to participate began his downfall. For worshiping God is one of the ways to get to know God. The more we worship the more we become intimate with God. Lucifer stayed so busy doing a good *duty,* or *works,* that in time the job (or *works*) defined him. It made him look good and it scratched his vain itch; an itch he would not have gotten if he had poured himself into worshiping God. Soon discontent with leading worship as God had made him to do, he wanted to be more than God had created him—he lusted after a much higher position. He saw how that after he had poured himself into his good work the angelic host was wanting more, excited for more, yelling, "more, more"! However, he had emptied himself into his job; he could not bring the angelic host to climax. He had maxed himself out and could have stayed there a 1000 years (*no, no wait, make that a trillion years*) but could not bring them any further into something they wanted, for it was not in him to give. Only when God would show up and the ecstasy of His presence would flood the host would they experience the fulfillment they had hungered for—God's awesome presence. This devotion lucifer witnessed coming from them to God, made him envious.

When God manifested His presence, lucifer would observe the angels and think something like this: "I can take him. I see nothing about him that I cannot handle. They just love him, or think they do, and think they want him. But, if he was not here for them to pour their devotion into then I could give them what they long for. This is just the way things are right now, but in time, I can change that, and they will receive from me. They refuse to receive from me since they think he is the stuff. He is just another six-dimensional being just like me."

God does not create dumb defective things so satan was not dumb he simply let his emotions guide his choices. I think an intelligent being as God created lucifer would be too smart to take on a God that he knew was as big as our God is. However, his blindness was a choice and his choices led him to a perverted perspective; much like a partial imagery does to our carnal, natural, physical-minded conclusions of spiritual scripture that demand a Spiritual helper to understand. Refusing to humble himself before such a God began to twist his thinking. He could have avoided his fall by getting to know God instead of just assuming, in his arrogance, that he had all knowledge, as some of our denominations assume today.

If God had manifested in His fullness each time He appeared in the 2nd heaven, lucifer's assumption would have been correct in the thinking that God was like him. However, a six-dimensional mind cannot contain an eleven-dimensional God. The angels can manifest themselves in our three dimensions and appear just like us as we see in this verse- **Be not forgetful to entertain strangers: for thereby some have entertained angels unawares (Hebrews 13:2)**. According to this verse, angels have been among us and we have been un-aware that we had been near a higher dimensional being. When they do manifest we can understand them in three dimensions but not as they really are in six dimensions. We would not know we are talking to someone who is actually a six-dimensional being, for he would not show his higher dimensions to us. Alternatively, I should say, to make this idea more clear, we cannot *see* into those other three dimensions, so we only see them in three dimensions. I think God is the same. He shows Himself where the angels could understand Him. He was not trying to hide anything from them. He just shows up and all they can see and measure is six dimensions, so they assume He is like them. Either way, they are only seeing part of Him. This would explain why lucifer could be so stupid when God had not created him stupid. His pride and arrogance stupefied him.

One day lucifer, while in his "star suite" (where he had placed his name on his own door with a star on it), looked in the first mirror ever invented, and knew he was looking at someone different than God had created. He saw vanity, jealousy, envy, strife, and dissatisfaction. As he thought it through, he realized how this "new him" had come to be; he had actually discovered something he was not really looking for. Just as Christopher Columbus inadvertently discovered America, lucifer had inadvertently discovered religion. It was a way he would be able to distract others and get them to think differently in subtle ways than God wanted them to, and to think his way, if possible. If not possible, at best, he could cloud the thinking with his perversions. Maybe he could use this to get his followers to think in ways that would serve him to the point the servers would

Jeremiah C. Southerman

be willing slaves and devote their lives to him. As the years, decades, or maybe centuries (*or maybe even a trillion years*) passed, he worked his plan, preached his doctrine, and watched the results on the few in order to refine his delivery to the many. He turned his genius into a twisted, perverted way of thinking; he became good at lying, deceiving, and spinning a story that seemed to fit the things easily visible to the distracted viewer. None of this caught God by surprise. For, above all things, God esteems free-will as important. He knew the only way to assure true loyalty from anyone would be to allow them the free-will to make their own choices, even if it meant He might lose some along the way. If lucifer and the angels wanted an alternative philosophy, then by all means, God had to allow it. Even if 100 percent of the angels rebelled against Him, it would be no threat to Him. Lucifer knew that the angels under his care would share his doctrine with the angels under the care of Gabriel and Michael. The angels (I will call them sheep for teaching purposes) under lucifer's care, would share his doctrine with the sheep under Gabriel and Michael's care. Thankfully those sheep followed protocol and went to their shepherds to ask about this new doctrine. Being lucifer's peers not his subordinates, Gabriel and Michael were not awestruck by his beauty and wisdom so they did not become deceived. Rather, they explained the truth to their "sheep", as good shepherds should, thereby saving them from wrong doctrine and eternal judgment. *It is my hope this book will do the same for you.*

What lucifer had come to desire was the worship. Not understanding the God-kind of worship, he wanted worship the same way we fallen-thinking humans would. So, if you have ever thought what it would be like to have someone bow down, kiss your feet, and give you more accolades than you currently know exist, and humble themselves before you as if they were dirt, these are the same "vain thoughts" or feelings that lucifer was after, just magnified. To achieve followers, which would eventually end in them worshiping him, he would have to begin to preach a subtle twist to God's truth before he could preach blatant rebellion. An example of a subtle twist to truth would be the following doctrine discussed in the next paragraph. It is not exactly wrong but neither is it truth. It is perverted a bit, so it steals and robs the believer and leaves them short of what God the giver wishes for the believer to receive. This is by no means all there is to

How God Got Mary Pregnant

say about this subject, I only hope to make a point, not teach this rabbit trail to its end. *Now for my next trick: I am about to make some people mad.*

Many churches have a saying, "We are just old sinners saved by grace." I can see why that doctrine is with us, but it robs us, and here is how. God knew before He made us that humanity would sin and die. God could not impose the entirety of the death sentence on us at the time of sin or there would be no family, which was the original reason for this plan of God…to get a family. God designed us so that when Adam sinned the soul would become dominate. He created us in a fashion that all three parts of us would work in unity according to the will of God, but only when we embrace His will as our own will, also. That responsibility was in our soul. Our spirit is the life source, but the soul is command central. The flesh is the house for the two, the "beast of burden" if you care to call it that, which carries us through our earthly sojourn. When Adam sinned, the spirit died that day and his soul and flesh deserved instant death but God provided a substitute, a critter, probably a lamb. It, the innocent critter, that did not reject God as Adam did, would have to die, shed its blood, give it's carnal life (it has no spirit life), to cover for mankind. This symbolic act would cover until someone (Jesus) could do for humankind what the critter could not do, which was pay a spiritual redemption price. During the long gap, humanity had a soul designed to dominate so that it could override (not change, but only temporarily override) the acts of a death nature and live more Godly that moment. That is why we see the righteous from the Old Testament in a place called paradise (not heaven). They overrode the pull of the flesh best as they could with no spiritual help, which proved that if spiritual salvation were available to them they would embraced it. Therefore, their faith was *counted* unto them as righteousness (much like credit). Even though they could not be *righteous* yet for that is of God and God had not come to earth as a man to re-open that door. The soul (mind) is where our will, intellect, emotions, dreams, hopes, plans and such originate. We all grow up having that soul trained by five physical senses, from which we get information. This information is carnal (that means it is *not spiritual)* and this incoming carnal information is corrupted and influenced by satan, a fallen spiritual being. Since we have been trained in this carnal way of thinking, our souls need retrained and washed by the

Word. The Word, which came from a Spiritual God who is not of this fallen world, knows all that is above our five senses- **Husbands, love your wives, even as Christ also loved the church, and gave himself for it; That he might sanctify and cleanse it with the washing of water by the word, That he might present it to himself a glorious church, not having spot, or wrinkle, or any such thing; but that it should be holy and without blemish. (Eph. 5:25-2).** The church is the born-again of the earth. Here we see that the born-again have spots and blemishes that need washed. It is not our born again spirit that needs washing because that new spirit came from God and is perfect, as we see here- **For by one offering he** (Jesus) **hath perfected for ever them** (you and me,) **that are sanctified** (*that is if you have done the Romans 10:9-10 thing*) **(Hebrews 10:14).** The new, born again spirit is what makes us brethren (and sisters) to Jesus. **For both he** (Jesus) **that sanctifieth and they** (you and me) **who are sanctified *are* all of one: for which cause he** (Jesus) **is not ashamed to call them brethren (Hebrews 2:11).** It is in our soul where the vanity (a blemish) still dwells. Our soul-mind still sins, because the flesh still pulls at it and it, our souls, give in from time to time. It happens because our soul was not born again; the desires within it must be steadily changed from what was, to what should be. That saying, "old sinner saved by grace", comes from only looking at our souls. It is a *soul saying*, so to speak, not a *spiritual saying*. It does not describe the *spiritual* part of a Christian, but it does describe the un-renewed parts of our souls. There is a war within us, we see in **1 Peter 2:11-Dearly beloved,** (he is talking to Christians here) **I beseech *you* as strangers and pilgrims,** (on an earth that is not our spiritual home) **abstain from fleshly lusts, which war against the soul;** Note that the body, "flesh", is at war with the "soul"/mind. Showing us that our body wants things that "feel good" but may be, and often are, bad for us (such as more candy and ice cream, or sex with our neighbor's wife or husband). Also, just as the body is at war with the soul, so the soul is at war with the spirit. In Romans 8;7 we are told the carnal mind, or the mind that thinks in carnal terms is at war, hostile, towards God. So, as long as we were spiritually dead (not born-again) our spirit, mind, and flesh all three cared not for right or wrong, but only what seemed to us at that moment to satisfy self. However, if you choose to accept Jesus your dead human spirit from Adam get replaced with a living human spirit from

Jesus, which makes you, spiritually speaking, "born again." Your soul now has a source to draw from that will not agree with the lustful adultery your flesh enjoyed. Until we grow in grace and knowledge- **But grow in grace, and *in* the knowledge of our Lord and Saviour Jesus Christ. To him *be* glory both now and for ever. Amen. (2 Peter 3:18)**- our souls will keep thinking that nothing has changed and that we are still just a sinner that went through a baptism or an altar call. The selfish trained soul likes this form of life, for it stays in charge with this old normal way of thinking. This is not walking in the spirit, for it is abnormal for our carnal mind to submit to the spiritual mind- **Be not double minded (James 1:8 and 4:8).** Instead, let the spiritual mind lead your soul and flesh- **Let this mind be in you, which was also in Christ Jesus: (Philippians 2:5).** To put into practice the submission of our carnal will to a God-lead spiritual will is a very hard thing to do because most people would rather take the easy road and coast into heaven with no reward. If a shepherd pushes his sheep they, generally speaking, find another church. The shepherds who excuse the wrong actions of the sheepeople by saying: "it's ok, after all you are just an old sinner saved by his grace" either do not know truth themselves (*they are ignorant*), or they do not to apply any pressure in the form of accountability to the sheepeople (*they are lazy*), or they fear if they do the tithes and offerings will go elsewhere (*they are greedy*). The Biblical truth is that- **For the law of the Spirit of life in Christ Jesus hath made me free from the law of sin and death. (Romans 8:2).** The truth is you do not *have* to sin, when you do it was a choice; all of our actions are a choice. Fleshly indulgence feels good regardless of our spiritual condition (sin still feels good to our flesh) if our spirit is alive or dead. It takes training our mind to think like His (which can only be found in His Word), that is why He gave the soul such strength so it could rule even a dead spirit. That is why you hear of people who were called "good people" but never were born again. They had parents that told them right from wrong. They evaluated what their parents taught intelligently, (using their soul) and concluded that dad and mom were right. Even if there were no God to answer to, to live the way "good parents" told us, makes for a better society.

As long as our soul can, it will keep the spirit serving it (remember the story from earlier in this book where we learned about keeping spirit/prince

Jeremiah C. Southerman

off the horseback while the soul/servant rides high in the saddle). We are more than just a soul housed in flesh, so that saying shortens, or takes away from, what Jesus has done for us, because it highlights, exalts, and gives emphasis to carnal things and ignores the spiritual (again, another carnal interpretation of a spiritual concept). How belittling to Jesus it is to carry the image that we are "just old sinners saved by grace" because it creates false humility in us. Because we do not know God or the Bible we *fear* (which is of satan by the way) offending God by declaring what His word actually says about us. Religion thrives on this and satan loves the fact that our ignorant, fallen, guilt-laden minds thinks that God surely did not mean what the Bible says. It must mean something else so we then proceed to attach our own carnal interpretations to it. If we dwell on that teaching and what that doctrine produces in our imagination then we see ourselves as just lowly worms. He also tells us in Romans 8:37 we are "more than conquerors" and in II Corinthians 5:17 he says- "**Therefore if any man** *be* **in Christ,** *he is* **a new creature: old things are passed away; behold, all things are become new**".

Our soul has had a leash around our spiritual neck, so to speak, leading us through life, and that, only if your parents taught us morals. If not, then we could be like hitler where your "dead spirit" leads your soul. Sadly, many of these soul-dominated doctrines are built into the Christian church. I will explain that also. God had to give humanity a set of rules (guardrails if you like) to keep us from going over the cliff again as they did before the flood of Noah's day or the people at Sodom and Gomorrah. That guardrail was the Law of Moses, which is Judaism, and a baseline of Christianity. This law was the leash God placed on the necks of the flesh of His chosen people, a people chosen to do a job. Religion continues to keep that soul-controlled leash on our spirit's neck. We relate to the rules because the rules are natural-based and carnal, like our un-renewed minds. Religion survives by keeping us from growing spiritually so we will continue to live by rules that our carnal minds can relate to. This is to live for the flesh, because our soul, in most cases, will side with our flesh (as doing the fasting experiment talked about earlier will show you). However, to walk in the spirit as Jesus did, things will be different- ***This*** **I say then, Walk in the Spirit, and ye shall not fulfill the lust of the flesh (Gal**

5:16). The ideal, then, would be to submit our souls to the spirit and hand the leash (or the reigns of the horse) over to the spirit. That is no small task because we are too carnal-minded to understand or trust that we should, but it should be our goal. We do this by renewing our soul, or our mind, by the Word, which begins to form a correct Godly spiritual image of our position. A position God Himself placed us in when we were born again. This constant pouring in of His word begins to remove our fallen, default, small, lower-state "I'm just a worm", point of view of ourselves (the false image of humility I was talking about). It begins to paint an image on the inside of us that inspires us to rise above what we have been most of our lives. It inspires us to stop engaging in things that are harmful to our spirits and souls. With due diligence, one will rise above the subtle lie that "we are *just* old sinners saved by grace" and come to recognize other subtle lies we have been deceived by.

Now that I have made some of you mad at me, let me brag on you a moment. It is true that most people who have been lead to believe *that* doctrine are still "good people". They have made it past a "stage one" mentality; they put their religion into practice and restrain their flesh (which is a good thing). Others, and this became big with the hippies and remains so today among that mindset, they only desire to live in a "stage one" mentality. A quick example of what I am talking about when I say "stage one" would be that flesh is the lowest form of our being—to please flesh is to practice the "if-it-feels-good-do-it" mentality. That is lowering us to nearly the level of dogs, (see God's attitude towards that in Ezekiel 23). People that are more intelligent, or choose to use the intellect God gave them lean towards engaging in things that deny the flesh but inspire the mind (they simply keep their body healthy and restrain it by practicing self-control). This is far better than stage one, this can be done Christian or not, you only have to be intelligent (*something hippies were not known for*). This level is where God wanted the old covenant Israelite's to live (i. e. with disciplined souls), just as many "good people" do today. God will give His blessing to that as much as He can. However, it is NOT walking in the spirit (call that "stage three" living). A person will not walk in the spirit unless they go on to "stage two" from "stage one". That is why religion has a place in this world. I would love to see you walk on past religion and into Jesus. If you are a Christian I would say walk *further* into Him. A common example of this would be that many teenagers who do not have a cause, that is, have a belonging tie to something bigger than themselves (a church group, a hobby, a sports team, a close family) are often "stage one". As they mature they get jobs, marry, have kids and other responsibilities, and if they can discipline themselves to remain there (*because their parents raised them right),* then they have, without thinking about it, become "stage two". It is my hope that people do not stop there with disciplined souls or at religion. Religion often takes the spot of where Jesus should be. And many a church leader WANTS that. Just like lucifer wanted what should have been Gods these cult/religious leaders (with satan's help) mentally on the soul level intercept a young Christians walk capture them in a sense to serve the cult/church/religion until they die, feeling good about their vain lives the whole time. God's desire is that we get past religion and walk in the spirit, as Jesus set the example. With time, effort, and denying our flesh and souls the lofty place they have always enjoyed, we will replace it by our understanding of our true victorious position in Christ, and we will have good results in rising above "the self" from that correct understanding. One day you will look back and realize many parts of your life is more dominated by the spirit, and not so much, so often, or so easily controlled by the leash in the hand of the carnal-minded soul. It can happen, for when we were born again our spirits became like His, as Adam's was before he fell, and like Jesus was all His life. He is a Spirit and He made us to worship (i. e. to be intimate with Him) on His spiritual level. We cannot achieve that spiritual level from our non-spiritual minds/souls. It must be done from our spirits, which are not "just old spirits saved by grace", but rather they are brand new, perfect, Holy, and of God's very essence. A short way to view all that is: a stage one person has flesh as *lord* of their lives. A stage two person has the soul as *lord* of their lives. A stage three person has the new born-again spirit as *lord* of their lives and that part of us is from Jesus and knows how (and desires to make) God *Lord* of our lives. So, anytime we Christians can force our soul to submit to our spirit-man we will be submitting to Jesus and walking in the spirit as He desires and instructs.

Two things in our souls that seem to be too big for nearly all humanity to overcome: sex and money. To possess money or engage in consensual sex, both shower the accolades, or adoration, on us from others that the un-renewed parts of our soul so desires. It is a sort of worship that we receive from others. I think this is the best glimpse we have of what lucifer was looking for. Today, when we see otherwise Godly men fall to sex and money, it is because they did not take the steps to be cleansed thoroughly of the area of weakness that led to these sins due to the pull of the flesh and the vanity in the soul. Our souls are cleansed by the "washing of the Word". As we "soak" in the Word to remove every "spot, wrinkle and blemish" from our character that He reveals to us during our time of "soaking". Do not misunderstand; our past is forgiven upon repentance of sin and confession of Christ Jesus. God most assuredly receives our spirit-man as His child and "seats us in heavenly places" with Him. He will never leave you nor forsake you when you sin out of weakness, for He knows the pull of the flesh and the vanity of the soul. He does not say in the Bible that you will never leave Him, He says He will never leave you. There is a difference you cant loose your salvation like you loose your keys but you can throw it away. However, the strength to overcome the pulls of the flesh and the worlds temptations is innate within our new spirit-man born inside us after you do the Romans 10:9-10 thing.

When we read about the temptation of Adam and Jesus, we discover both times that satan was trying to appeal to their vanity. Satan figured Jesus had some, but he figured wrong. Vanity and pride are so similar they are nearly indistinguishable from each other, and it seems to be the deepest part of our perversion. The perversion runs so deeply, that God even addresses it, in a fashion, to let us know it is never purged, just steered. He says- **"Humble yourselves therefore under the mighty hand of God, that he may exalt you in due time" (I Peter 5:6).** He never actually tells us to frustrate ourselves by focusing on the purging of vanity, as He instructs us in the commandment, "thou shalt not steal". The purging of vanity that happens is a by-product of spiritual growth, which He does tell us to focus on. He will take care of, or scratch our vanity for us, if we "humble ourselves that *He* may exalt us" as we seek Him, grow in Him, and exalt Him. If satan, or we, or anyone other than God, exalts us, then we are set up for a fall. If we allow satan to promote us, then he can tear us down, he can have his way much easier in our lives if we are not humbling ourselves before God and busy our lives with chasing vanities.

God is not vain in the worship of Him. It is more akin to a loving married man and wife sharing sexual intercourse instead of rape, molestation and/or prostitution. Prostitutes do "duty" its their "job". Much like satans job was to oversee the worship but never got intimate with it. For with God, it is giving in two directions, not just taking. He knew what He was doing when He set up sex and marriage. Marriage is preaching a part of the gospel in that a man and wife are sharing on two levels:#1) our flesh bodies, and#2) our souls/minds where our emotions and memories are stored. Sex between married couples (one male and one female) is a type of worship of, an honoring, a paying homage to, each other. With worship of God, it is also on two levels, but consists of our souls/minds and our *spirits*. The flesh interests Him not, it is the spirit that makes alive (John 6:63). The same way it is a man's greatest desire to share his life, to share of himself, and inject his very essence into this wife, it is, likewise God's greatest desire to inject Himself, His very essence, into His church, the Bride. Moreover, just as a husband and wife's greatest joy is to bring forth "fruit" of her womb of his seed, likewise, it is God's greatest joy for us as members of the body of the church, His Bride, to bring forth spiritual fruit. Our small minds struggle with the concept that a church with many members (about half male) is a bride to a Spirit Being. But, His thoughts are higher than our thoughts. He says- **"And there came unto me one of the seven angels which had the seven vials full of the seven last plagues, and talked with me, saying, Come hither, I will shew thee the bride, the Lamb's wife" (Revelation 21:9).** Later in the book, He says, **And the Spirit and the bride say, Come. And let him that heareth say, Come. And let him that is athirst come. And whosoever will, let him take the water of life freely" (Revelation 22:17).** Our new, born-again spirits become one with Him. That is what the Old Testament "Day of Atonement" was picturing- **Also on the tenth day of this seventh month there shall be a day of atonement: it shall be an holy convocation unto you; and ye shall afflict your souls,** (by fasting) **and offer an offering made by fire unto the LORD (Lev. 23:27).** This day pictured a time in their future, our present, that a human (*if you choose to do the Romans*

10:9-10 thing) could become one with God (in spirit, and later fully body and soul). That is part of what Jesus did for us when He atoned for the sin we could not atone for and that gave us the ability to be "At-one-ment" in spirit, with Him. Therefore, to worship Him is to give Him a chance to give Himself away, which pleases Him greatly. To worship satan is to feed his twisted vanity, and in the end, he will eat you like a black widow spider (*and to think tree huggers worship fallen nature?*).

In order for satan to have the worship he desired, he had to dethrone God. Then he, in his twisted thinking, thought he could satisfy that vain hunger within himself, thinking something like, "Only if Jehovah would not come out on the stage, I could somehow get the angelic host to bow and prostrate themselves willingly before me the way they do when God manifests His presence."

In satan's thinking, he could have the angels spilling their emotions, dancing in the aisles, taking off their bras, and throwing them................... on............... the ....stage ....Wait, wait....................... ah, hum........? I reckon angels do not have bras. Isn't it interesting, though, to consider where that idea/action came from? What would possess women at a concert, listening to, and dancing to, the music to get that emotionally involved with what they are hearing to engage in such activity?.......... huh can you say, "rock and roll"? .. wonder if there could be a spiritual connection to satan's realm? God seems to have built into us the desire to give ourselves away, to expose ourselves to (to not hide from) the person we desire. The women are giving an *offering* of sorts to the thing (in this case, music or the band creating the music, and to the spiritual realm— *the wicked spirit* behind the music) that has so stirred their emotions (*I know, I know*, not *all* rock music is bad, and this happens not *only* at rock concerts). This action is much like a wife undressing to give an offering of her body to her husband. Satan has learned how to draw on this built-in desire to worship, or belong to, something bigger than ourselves, and we have witnessed his perversion of it. In the case of the rock-n-roll-concert-emotional frenzy, satan gets to be the rock star here on earth that he once used to be there in heaven's worship, but this time he actually gets what he wanted then; perverted worship. Ironically, these rock stars that our society refers openly to as "idols" receive such "worship" from their fans. Look at the destructive ways and destructive things these "idols" produce, and note that all this is on the emotional level, which is a carnal level, no spiritual life in it, or even logical living in it. Emotionally (body and soul) we are influenced by these "idols", while our spirits are not. What does God say about carnality? **"For to be carnally minded *is* death; but to be spiritually minded *is* life and peace. Because the carnal mind *is* enmity** (hostile) **against God: for it is not subject to the law** (or ways) **of God, neither indeed can be" (Romans 8:6-7).** That is because the ways of God are spiritual, not carnal. We see lucifer, created to make music, allowing perversion into his thinking and then the perversion transform him into satan the devil. From fallen perverted humanity, satan gets the worship his perverted mind wanted back then, but now from carnal people, not spiritual ones. Hum? Reckon God did a good job creating a music man if the music man could be that powerful with his music.

So back to the saga. To get what satan wanted (back then, before there were humans) he tried a coup, but it failed. Jesus said in Luke 10:18-...**I beheld Satan as lightning fall from heaven...** indicating how fast God threw him out of heaven. As I stated above, if 100 percent of the angelic host rebelled against God, He needed to do nothing but wave of His hand to wipe out their best-laid plans. Nevertheless, neither God nor satan was finished. God was going to use satan in His plan and satan was going to attempt plan B to get himself a kingdom (he never knew humans were in the future plans when he made his first attempt). Now, to make it clear, God never had a plan B since He knows the future and He knew what was going to happen. The Bible tells us that Jesus was counted as slain from the very beginning- **And all that dwell upon the earth shall worship him, whose names are not written in the book of life of the Lamb slain from the foundation of the world (Revelation 13:8).** For something to be counted as if it happened before the universe in which it happened existed, demands that "the Someone" who was seeing the happening happen before-hand, had to be higher/bigger/above the universe in which the happening was going to happen. So, before anything happens to your brain I will hush my happenings and look further into the mechanics of what happened. (*I bet everybody reads that one twice*)

How God Got Mary Pregnant

God lives outside of time and space so He could see all of time and space before His creation (*do not ask me how, I do not know—He is just that big*). He looked into time and saw that regardless of whichever probability, time line, or, for you physics buffs out there— God looked into the "many worlds"— or as Michio Kaku calls it the "multiverse" and God saw Adam in every parallel universe always rejecting His leadership. As a side note: What Mr Kaku has spent years theorizing on, using his mind and mathematics, is in itself a demand of the "imagery" put forth in the Bible. What I mean by that is that somethings are never said in the Bible, but when you consume enough of it an image builds inside you and without words you have a knowing that something that can be put into words is already in scripture in image form. Such as the critter God killed to cloth Adam and Eve was a lamb. The Bible never says so but imagery pretty much demands it. Same as scripture pretty much demands a multiverse. Now back to the flow of our saga.

However, as God looked further than Adams sin into the future, He saw many sons and daughters of Adam that had the potential to be born into His (God's) family. Since Adam corrupted the beginning of each of the time lines, all the sons and daughters inherited that corruption of sin. Therefore, in order to have a family, God had to allow them to go through sin before they would come back to Him. However, when they came back, they would not want to stray ever again for they would know that God has it all, and there is nothing elsewhere for them; that daddy's house is where they want to be. This is much like our teenagers who rebel or stray a few years, then come back and live as we counseled them when they were younger (younger, as in way back when they "*knew everything*"). Another example of this would be the prodigal son in Luke 15:11-32.

That is why He put man on earth with satan because satan's philosophy was the alternative to God's ways. God wanted to allow everyone a choice. That way He could weed out the culls before the finalization of His kingdom. Since satan chose a self-philosophy (and developed it in doctrinal form) God was able to use satan for His purpose, knowing that He would win some and lose some. Think of it like this: God is not wicked to put human-kind with a devil-kind for testing. This way God and the free-will

53

Jeremiah C. Southerman

human who must choose whether to reject God or not, both God and the person will know that a trillion years after they have been with Him in the family that they will not become the next lucifer. Otherwise, the whole messy thing will have to play out many times before all the people remaining know for sure they wish to be there with God. I think He is an off-the-chart genius to do it aforetime as He did. He wanted man to have a choice or He would not have placed the tree of the knowledge of good *and* evil in the garden. God never made evil, satan is the author of it. God created all "things", but evil is a concept and a way of thinking—it is not a created *thing*. God hates sin and the effects of it, but He had to allow the option.

Since the option to not allow us an option was not an option for God since He wanted kids that He knew wanted Him. He knew He would have to buy back, or redeem us, His kids. All of humanity that wanted to be redeemed, that is. These redeemed would be the ones that thought God's offer was a good deal. *What do you think? (Your name here),*_____. But, why would He have to buy us back? Today, if you and I only have to look up to heaven, acknowledge that Jesus is Lord, confess Him as savior, and bingo! we are saved, then why could God just not do that for Adam when Adam said, "Ah…, ah, hey father I messed up, can I come back into where I once was?" Even though Adam and God both wanted that, it just could not be that easy. For one thing, God was no longer Adam's father, for God is the father of our spirits. When Adam rejected a Spirit God as his father, he also reduced God's status to only creator and advisor in his life, not family. Why could God not just allow that? A Presbyterian deacon and I used to discuss this question with each other. Our question was, "Why did blood have to be shed?" "Why did Jesus have to die?" I have since lost contact with this deacon, but I now have the answer, and here is the short version: God did not have full Authority………………….. (Pause …………………….. let that sink in a moment)……………. This is another example of imagery that is "written" between the lines, so to speak. This disagrees with most mainstream teaching that says "God crushed Jesus" or "God demanded death to pay for sin." While that is kind-of true (*a little bit*), I do not agree completely with that idea. I disagree with the presentation because it leaves a negative

How God Got Mary Pregnant

image of God behind in the minds of believers and it paints God as an angry God who is so mad that He is going to kill someone, even if His own "beloved son" gets in His way (Matt. 3:17; 17:15; Mark 1:11; 9:7). As if God is so mad that He is going to kill off humanity before the universe they live in dies of old age (*entropy rules*). As if God wants revenge, so He is going to kill them all to satisfy a personal blood lust He has. As if Jesus loved us so much more than Jehovah, He decided to come to our rescue, thereby becoming one of us and trades His perfect life for our imperfect lives to save us from an angry God.

That is the resulting image from the doctrine taught from many a pulpit in Christendom. That does not fit with "God is love" (1 John 4:8, 16). God is the author of life. To kill is not love, but to let evil live is not love either, so He had to deal with evil. Unfortunately, death was the only way. Therefore, He did not *demand* death be the price, death *had* to be the price; God had no choice if He wanted to have His family. The Bible confirms this when we are told in scripture that Jesus asked, "If it be possible let this cup pass from me" (Matt 26:39). God at Jesus request in that prayer looked into the miltiverse once more to see if He and The Word just by chance had missed something a trillion years before man was created. Again this is an imagery pulled from the depths of scripture. If Jesus was a Deity on earth (which He was not) then He would know that there was no other way, that He and Jehovah had already looked into the multiverse and saw the future. Jesus the MAN was hoping, just hoping, another way had been found in His 33 years of life. Which I am going to take it a step farther and say that is another *proof* that Mr Kaku is correct. I say that because Jesus would know that there would be billions, no make that trillions, of universe born into existence in the 33 years of His life and He was hoping one could contain and *out* for the hell He was about to go through when He ask can this cup pass... Now back to the saga: If the cup passed from Him, it would have passed back to humanity and we all would have to pay for our own sin. That would be a break-even deal, with nothing left over to qualify us to pass into His kingdom. However death was the only way and if we are dead from paying for our sins then where is Gods family? If we were dead satan can't get his kingdom but he successfully kept God from getting His. That is why we see satan trying to lead spiritually dead humanity back to the tree of life so that man could live forever in our fallen state which would give satan his kingdom. God stopped that plan, more on that later. Through the deception of Eve and the rebellion of Adam and God stopping satan from the tree of life God wanted them back so satan the kidnapper named his price. He set a "perfect blood" price on humanity's head, satan knew there was no "perfect blood" anywhere in the universe (based on his limited seven-dimensional point of view, that is), so he figured he had God cornered. Further, as one meditates, one sees it is a violation of total imagery to think that God would put a "ransom" price of death on His own head. How foolish! This is the stupidity of religion, listen to the thought process in that doctrine: "*I, God, am going to create man whom I know will sin before I create them, and I will hate sin so much, that I will demand that I die to buy them back for myself. And when I get there to pay the price I demanded, I will ask me if I have to go through with this or can I allow that cup to pass from myself.*" That is why satan figured he had God cornered. In his ignorance of how big God is, he did not know God could do such a thing as shed perfect blood—blood that God did not have. And, satan never dreamed God would then die, and raise *himself* from the dead. (note the italics, more on that later)

Where I do agree with the mainstream presentation is in that there *was* anger flowing from the throne of God *towards sin*. God loved the sinner but not the sin. God had pre-established that sin had to be annihilated, but therein was a problem; the annihilation would require the soul of a man, "for the soul that sins shall die" (Ezek. 18:4). Without a soul, you are equal to a dog— dogs do not go to heaven. Man was so wrapped up in, entangled in, and intimate with sin, that man could not be separated from sin without the separation killing him. He needed someone who could separate the soul and body, thereby redeeming the souls (and making a way for the soul to rejoin a living spirit) instead of being tied to a dead spirit that was headed for hell, and flesh that was headed back to the dust in which it came. That living spirit qualifies the redeemed to enter into the perfect domain of God's third heaven without the light of the third heaven annihilating the dark spirit that indwells the unredeemed human. This worked well to fulfill the legal demands of a vile kidnapper that was in the process of holding God's kids captive. It was not a case of the

How God Got Mary Pregnant

kidnapper saying, "If you do not deliver the money by this time, at this location, I will kill them." This kidnapper had already done his job of "spiritual killing" in the Garden of Eden, where he separated Adam from the source of spiritual life. The mortal wound would send them all to an eternal separation to be with the kidnapper in eternal torment unless *the Someone* paid the ransom. As a result of the original "spiritual killing" done in the garden, the humans that were to have been God's kids were being born dead and needed to be born-again, which satan did not understand could be done. In the absorption of God's anger towards sin, the demands of the Law of Moses were also satisfied. The law only pointed us towards our need for a hero, but the Hero that stood in the gap for humanity did not survive the heroic act as one of us. A just God could not allow death and hell to hold the guiltless, so He raised Jesus up from hell. But no longer one of us, He is a glorified human with a body no longer from Adam and with the dual citizenship Adam never grabbed hold of. Adams invitation to salvation was the fruit of a tree the tree of life. Jesus is our tree of life, our invitation is often an alter-call at a church an internet, tv or radio preacher encouraging the listener to confess Jesus as Lord. Adam was in an "alive" state from his creation, unlike us. He was NOT born again as we are once we do the Romans 10:9-10 thing. He had an advantage over us in that he did not have a dead spirit pulling him towards sin, he had other advantages also more on that later, right now lets look further into what he did to us and some of the story of what Jesus did to fix the mess Adam put us in.

The book of Ruth gives us insight to the redemption story. Please go right now and read the book of Ruth (*all four short chapters of it*). I want to use a few verses to show my point. Again, this is imagery at work. In the book of Ruth this is an insight to behind-the-scenes in the spirit realm, or maybe in the garden after God was discussing Adam's mistake with Adam. God told Adam that his domain was contaminated and needed redeemed. Adam's repentant attitude was to do so, but he had not yet realized how badly he had messed up until the Logos explained it further. Adam, not being Deity, did not know his offspring as God knew us a trillion years before we were born, so Adam was thinking only of the real estate he could "see" (understand) with his carnal understanding. This will be Ruth 4:4-6: **And I** The Logos, *the One that will become Jesus*, **thought to advertise**

Jeremiah C. Southerman

thee, Adam **saying, Buy** with the price of perfect blood *it* your domain that I gave you, that you foolishly gave to satan **before the inhabitants, and before the elders of my people. If** you Adam **wilt redeem *it*, redeem *it*: but if thou wilt not redeem *it*,** for you Adam are the one in control of it, but if not *then* **tell me,** for you have authority here, Adam **that I** The Logos/Jesus **may know: for *there is* none** (no other human) **to redeem *it* beside thee; and I** Jesus as a human *am* **after thee** (chronologically). Since Adam was thinking only of the creation God gave him (i. e. "*it*") and not the souls (i. e. "*them*") that were in his future, **And he** Adam **said, I will redeem *it*. Then said Boaz,** The Logos/Jesus said. **What day thou buyest** pay the redemption price **the field** (the earth,) **of the hand of Naomi,** (humanity) **thou must buy** "Redeem" *it* **also** all of humanity **of Ruth the Moabitess, the wife of the dead, to raise up the name of the dead upon his inheritance.** This speech here by Boaz, is a picture of the authority that humanity has under God. Adam had the first right, or first option, to redeem the creation and his offspring, but Adam could not redeem us, so Christ becomes the redeemer. **And the kinsman** Adam **said,** after The Logos explained the mess he had caused, **I cannot redeem *it* for myself,** I do not qualify, I have no perfect blood, **lest I mar mine own inheritance:** Because what you are telling me God, is, I will not be here to go on with physical life to build an inheritance for me or You, if I shed my blood for my own sin which will not count anyway. So you Logos/ Jesus **redeem thou my right to thyself; for I cannot redeem *it*.**

Some of you purest need to go grab your nitro pills, for I am about to disagree (just slightly) with the King James version. I am going to ask you to go back, re-read that last section, and drop the words added by the King James translators. Mainly, the word "*it*", because "*it*" was added by King James to give clarity to their point, a legitimate point, that ties the events of Ruth-Boaz-Naomi and the un-named kinsman to the statutes of the nation of ancient Israel (Numbers 5:8 and 27:11). For by adding the word "*it*" causes our naturally carnal minds to lean towards, think of, picture the imagery of a natural thing— land. That was one purpose of the statute for the nation of Israel back then. That statute was to protect family land, and the King James team saw that and tied the two together for us. I have come to understand that there is more to the story, which I have given you above.

How God Got Mary Pregnant

Now, for clarity, re-read the teaching this time dropping the words in gray italics, for that was King James addition. Below I have printed it without either King James insertion or mine. The imagery changes from talking about real estate to the souls of humanity. You can see that God is using imagery to teach us more/again/repeating this all-important truth about what He is doing for fallen humanity. Again this is God, the Logos, who would become Jesus 4000 years after this conversation, talking to Adam the first man who is about to begin the human race, in a fallen spiritual state, who will be in need of spiritual redemption. Naomi represents all of fallen humanity and Ruth represents the church that becomes Jesus' (Boaz in the story) bride, and Adam the kinsman closer than Boaz/Jesus to fallen humanity and the thing to be redeemed are the souls of humanity... **And I thought to advertise thee, saying, Buy before the inhabitants, and before the elders of my people. If thou wilt redeem, redeem, but if thou wilt not redeem tell me, that I may know: for there's none to redeem beside thee; and I after thee. And he said, I will redeem. Then said Boaz, What day thou buyest the field of the hand of Naomi, thou must buy also of Ruth the Moabitess, the wife of the dead, to raise up the name of the dead upon his inheritance. And the kinsman said, I cannot redeem for myself, lest I mar mine own inheritance: redeem thou my right to thyself; for I cannot redeem.**

Jesus did redeem humanity and the church that comes out of humanity will become the bride of Jesus, just as Ruth became the bride of Boaz. Note in verse 10 it says (cutting into the flow of the verse)…Ruth the Moabitess, the wife of Mahlon, have I purchased to be my wife, to raise up the name of the dead upon his inheritance, that the name of the dead be not cut off... Mahlon means "sick". Ruth was tied to "sickness" until death did part her and sickness. In the same way, we are tied to our flesh until death parts us. In the story, sickness (Ruth's husband) has died and she is free to marry another. If you have done the Romans 10:9-10 thing, then in the spirit realm your old, dead, fallen human, spirit has been buried with Christ. Col. 2:12 and Rom. 6:4 tells us we are... **Buried with him in baptism, wherein also ye are risen with *him* through the faith of the operation of God, who hath raised him from the dead.** Now back to the flow of the story…

Jeremiah C. Southerman

For satan, plan B was to get God's newest creation, man, to follow him. The volley was on. God explained to Adam what His way was and spent time with man before He allowed satan his best shot. And imagery tells me this took 30 years, I later learned, nearly 15 years after I had put "30 years" in my Bible study notes of the Hebrew word Berisheet which agrees with the image I that had built inside me real close. When satan got his chance, and we know the story, Eve believed the lies the serpent told her and ate of the wrong tree. Adam observed her "dead" and had to decide if dead was a bad thing or even real, since no one had ever died before. Adam arrogantly decided to rely on his intellect his logical mind and what he could see and touch with his five senses instead of God's words; explaining to Adam all the things not to do during their times of communing in the garden. The serpent's words seemed to line up well with what Adam's five senses told him, so he decided to rebel against what he knew God had told him, and decide for himself right and wrong — much like us when God says, "thou shalt not", and we rebel and go do the thing we were told not to.

God told Adam that if he ate of the tree, he would die- **But of the tree of the knowledge of good and evil, thou shalt not eat of it: for in the day that thou eatest thereof thou shalt surely die (Gen. 2:17).** Then we see that Adam ate- **And when the woman saw that the tree *was* good for food, and that it *was* pleasant to the eyes, and a tree to be desired to make *one* wise, she took of the fruit thereof, and did eat, and gave also unto her husband with her; and he did eat (Gen. 3:6).** *For more clarity on the story, read Genesis chapters 2 and 3... several times.*

At this point in the saga, humanity is separated from God, the author of life. Man, created to be an eternal spiritual being, is still an eternal being, and will be always. However, after sin entered the equation, unregenerate man was no longer be a spiritual being in God's likeness and God's image. But became a dark pervert distorted version of what God had created. We are an eternal being, housed in a temporary flesh body, when death finally takes the body, our immortal soul goes to be with our eternal spirit. Think of it like a flower or tree limb cut from the source of its life. It is dead at that moment but does not show the death until later (that is our flesh, it has death working in it). It has a soul in it also, a soul that bridges the gap between the

60

How God Got Mary Pregnant

flesh and spirit. This "soul/bridge" can be conformed to any way of thinking. The soul cares only for the evidence placed before it—it cares neither for God nor for man, only evidence. That is how Eve was deceived; she believed satan's interpretation of the evidence before her carnal eyes *(for more imagery on this, see the parable of the unjust judge in Luke 18:1-8)*.

Adam did not believe satan's deception; he simply made a choice to rebel. That choice affected all of humanity thereafter because it separated humanity from *real* life (as defined by God). Therefore, the eternal spirit of humanity was doomed to exist in a state defined as dead forever separated from God who made us, unless something reversed this. If separated from God, the only other alternative was satan for he is a spirit being also. He is just a dark evil spirit that God defines as "dead" who has his own eternal spiritual kingdom of death, hell, torture, misery, and so forth. Both kingdoms will last forever because they are spiritual, unlike the kingdoms of men that are physical and temporary. The kingdoms of men have an end. *(entropy rules)* Even if God and satan were to walk away and forget that our universe existed and the Bible never told us the end (a fiery one according to 2 Peter 3:10), we as physical beings would still have no future in eternity, because entropy/death rules the physical universe.

Now back to the saga. Satan thinks he has won the war against God. God had provided an alternative tree called "the tree of life" (which by the fact that Adam had not already gone to this tree earlier in his life shows us that he had not accepted God's "way" yet). Adam was still sinless, but he had not embraced Gods righteousness. His unwillingness to embrace Godliness left him in a fully human position, albeit a lofty human position, relative to ours today. He was still perfect and sinless but still very much in need of God's higher, divine input, much like our need for help in understanding God's instructions today. If we reject the Helper—the Holy Spirit—it will not void our eternal inheritance with Him. We will still maintain our lofty positions Jesus has purchased for us, but it leaves us more susceptible to satanic influence in our doctrines and choices. Please let us learn from Grandpa Adam! Once Grandpa Adam sinned, God had to protect fallen humanity from eating of the tree of life and living forever in his fallen, sick, and perverted state. It was an act of love and mercy for God to allow our flesh to die.

God only had one child at the time, a son, Adam. Eve and all others are "in" and "from" Adam. Eve was Adam's wife, not God's daughter. She got her living spirit from her husband Adam, not from God. Adam and Eve had built into them the ability to give life, to pass their life onto others, and to make others in their image. The only problem is now the image is distorted, twisted, and perverted. God could wipe them out and start over but He loves them. That would be like one of us killing our kids for getting in a cookie jar after we told them not to. God is higher than we are, so God already saw all the future with all of us in it, and He already loved us/you. (*Your name here, again*)_____. So, just as it would be foolish of us to kill our kids to fix a discipline problem, it would be foolish for God to start over with a new child, for love is there for the child, rebellion and all. God does not want to lose Adam and Eve because He cannot replace *them* (much like one of us losing one of our kids to a premature death). So now, the kids are half-dead (they still have physical life for a while). *For more imagery on half-dead, see the story of the Good Samaritan in Luke 10:30-35.* Meanwhile, the devil has kidnapped the children, and as kidnappers do, he wanted a ransom- **Even as the Son of man came not to be ministered unto, but to minister, and to give his life a ransom for many (Matt 20:28).** In addition, we read, **For *there is* one God, and one mediator between God and men, the man Christ Jesus; Who gave himself a ransom for all,** (all, who will do the Romans 10:9-10 thing) **to be testified in due time (I Timothy 2:5-6).**

We see in the book of Job a glimpse of how satan thought when he was negotiating for the right to tempt and torture Job- **And Satan answered the LORD, and said, Skin for skin, yea, all that a man hath will he give for his life (Job 2:4).** The devil was considering that now fallen man (which Job was) would only consider this flesh life as real life. Therefore, when the devil said "skin for skin" in Job's time, it reveals to us more of what satan is and how he thinks. Going back to his negotiating for Adam and Eve, it seems he was saying to God, "blood for blood," but then laughed at his seeming wisdom. *"Oh what am I saying God, you have no blood, I have the only two blood creatures in the universe, and guess what? Now they will have children for me and populate my kingdom! Fool! I win after all. I got my kingdom and you lost yours!"*

How God Got Mary Pregnant

Little did satan know that love had already found a way to pay the ransom price, for satan could not conceive of a Love that would shed itself of the Deity that he, satan, so desired, and come to earth as one of these human beings. In addition, satan failed to understand that God knew his future just as He does ours in our lower dimensions.

This marvelous plan of agape love and the third heaven are things satan does not understand. The Greek has more words to describe the true depth of things than our English language. For example, "agape" is Greek for the highest form of love; it means more than our English word love—even more than the way a mother loves her baby. From agape in the 11th dimension is where the plan of God was conceived and from there God could do just what satan the kidnapper had demanded, shed His blood (His innocent/perfect blood). Some people choke on the concept that satan could force Almighty God's hand. However, this was not satan forcing God's hand, it was God's love for us and dealing with Adams stupidity. If God was going to go on with the plan of getting His kids born into His family on a spiritual level, then God was bound to honor satan's demand. He had to honor that demand because He had to honor the dominion He had given humanity. Therefore, satan had a rightful (or legal) position he could "bargain" from and demand a price. As a conniving, self-centered pig, satan was thinking that God could not meet his demands. That there would be no way God could, since God had no blood or would (even if he had blood) shed that blood and die and submit Himself to satan to save these two flesh beings (he could not see the billions of us as God could see). Therefore, he set a "blood price" thinking, who could pay the price? In satan's limited mind, no one could. Again, he could not fathom that kind of love; it is beyond his seven-dimensional, perverted, fallen, evil abilities. Agape love; what a wonderful attribute of our God!

That brings us back to Mary's boy, the Word, who became flesh. The words of the Bible are *alive* in the spiritual realm. Meaning they actually "move, manipulate, change" things "over there" in the spirit realm, which affects things "over here" in the fallen physical arena. They give peace to the tormented, hope to the hopeless, sight to the blind, build happy marriages, heal sickness, make one wise, and so on. The book does not breathe, but two thousand years ago the essence of the book took on breath and lived in a body. The Word manifested as a human. The "book" had legs, a beard, and walked about for 33 ½ years doing before human eyes what it (the Word, the Bible, the book) is capable of doing still today. We have four eyewitness accounts of His events, that would be the four gospel books: Mathew, Mark, Luke, and John. Jesus, the Word—the Book— manifested as a human with all the power of the book two thousand years ago. Today it sits on our coffee tables as words with potential power. Our spiritual ignorance stops it from manifesting for us what it did for Him then. And, it is our religious traditions that our physical minds (our souls) can understand that supports our ongoing ignorance. We see the book as just that, only a book. However, it is *alive* with power. It is the most powerful thing on the planet, but religion has done a good job of blinding us so that we cannot tap into its power.

By the fact that we have so many Christian denominations is proof that we are messed up in our thinking. Divisions among us are based on heresy within us, and could be eliminated if we would truly seek Him and not our own glory. He is truth, and as we grow and mature in Him we should be in one accord as the disciples were in the upper room, rather than split, broken, and divided as the Body of Christ is today. Too many think they are teaching true doctrine — doctrine they did not learn of the Teacher, the Holy Spirit— by sitting at His feet in humility. They have learned their doctrine by reading denominational handbooks, not God's book. The book of Acts and the first 100 years of church history show us the power of being in one accord. The vanity of men has gone before you and me (for 1900 years) and set the course of many of our doctrines. We have remained on that course because of a lack of understanding that it is relationship with God the Father, Jesus the Son, and our Teacher, the Holy Spirit, that creates the faith that the power we see in the book of Acts to flow through. These vain doctrines started while the apostles were still alive; here are a few examples: Phil. 1:15-16, II John 1:7-10, III John 1:9 Gal. 1:6-9, Gal. 3:1 II Tim 4:14 and the book of Jude. Paul was often running into polluted doctrine when he went back to visit a church he had started. However, it is still our choice, so choose today to change your course. I do not adhere to any denominational doctrine, for

How God Got Mary Pregnant

denominations are of men. The term "birds of a feather flock together" fits denominationalism. Religion is a comfort zone. We should be Jesus freaks, disciples of Him, and students of the Bible. It should be our passion. Jesus even said- **"I am the bread of life". Your fathers did eat manna in the wilderness, and are dead. This is the bread which cometh down from heaven, that a man may eat thereof, and not die. I am the living bread which came down from heaven: if any man eat of this bread, he shall live forever: and the bread that I will give is my flesh, which I will give for the life of the world. The Jews therefore strove among themselves, saying, how can this man give us *his* flesh to eat? Then Jesus said unto them, Verily, verily, I say unto you, Except ye eat the flesh of the Son of man, and drink his blood, ye have no life in you. Whoso eateth my flesh, and drinketh my blood, hath eternal life; and I will raise him up at the last day (John 6:48-54).** If we all partook of Him, i. e. consumed the Bible voraciously and what it tells us to do, then we would not have denominational splits, and angry debates, even wars. The "religion" of Christianity is *almost* owned by satan, and none of the other religions are a threat to him. By this I mean he has influenced so many of our doctrines that his hand of perversion can be seen in many of them. The shallow doctrines of too much of Christendom are easily understood by our carnal minds, many leading us away from what God really wants. We are told by "religionist" (*I invent words*) that we need help understanding the Bible (we do…God's help), but aggressive greedy humans prey on that void in us by telling us they have an inside tract to God. Our belief in their lies comes from ignorance of God's truths because we (in the western world anyway) are too lazy to read the Bible enough to know for ourselves. This scenario has been repeated by other aggressive men in some other place, some other time, and men with demonic applause birth another denomination/cult. Christianity is a family in which you were born into, it was never meant to be a religion. You join a religion, a club, a cult, a team, a movement, a gang, etc.

The verses about eating His flesh continues from there but these verses make my point, especially verse 53. You are getting a small taste of "His flesh"; you just consumed a small part of His word, you just fed your spirit some spiritual food when you read His words…and He is The

Jeremiah C. Southerman

Word. So, what is it about Mary's little boy? This Word/Jesus character, and the uniqueness of His name? Why did He tell us to eat His flesh? The carnal, physical mind automatically thinks of cannibalism when we hear that, and that is what the Jews thought (vs. 52.) Moreover, some ignorant denominations teach today that the sacraments taken at communion become His actual flesh and blood, which *is* teaching their converts that they *are* cannibals because eating human flesh *is* cannibalism. Again, that is an example of partial imagery doing what it does best; causing error in doctrine that leads to division among the Body of Christ, and the followers of it farther from truth.

DOMINION

Now, we will go back and revisit Gen. 1:26, where God said let us make man in our image and give him dominion. This time focus on the word "dominion". Here is the definition from <u>Strong's Concordance:</u> A primitive root; to *tread* down, that is, *subjugates*; specifically to *crumble* off (come to, make to) have dominion, prevail against, reign, (bear, make to) rule, (-r, over), take. I have searched the Bible and cannot find anywhere that God took that dominion back after Adam sinned. Once He placed it in man's hands; it belongs to men. God did not give it conditionally. He simply gave it over, and only a man had the right to take it back from satan. Adam had the right but no longer the power, he lost the backing of the power of God to now do or perform what humanity wanted performed, but the right to that dominion stayed with man. Adam locked God out, but then realized his mistake and invited God back in. However, the damage was done—God could not just come back in His fullness, but was willing to do all He could. In God's discussion and explanation to Adam in the garden, as I discussed earlier from the book of Ruth, Adam agreed to give God as much control as possible for the redemption of humanity, which is where God's sovereignty comes in. This was similar to God's agreement with Abraham about his personal offspring, the nation of Israel, God cannot make any of Adam's offspring cooperate with Him to bring them back to where Adam

Jeremiah C. Southerman

wished he had left them in the beginning. Adam was saying to God, "I, as the authority figure on earth, give you permission to do what you need to do to redeem my offspring." God could not just bring them back into His presence because His full manifestation to "dead" creatures would have annihilated them. It would have been the same way turning on a light in a dark room annihilates the darkness. The spiritual, or parent force, inside humanity had lost connection to life and power of the spiritual force (i. e. God) so there was no power in humanity any longer to rule spiritually. The spiritual ruler, satan, could not make humanity sin, their soul was still subject to their command. However, humanity no longer had the ability to resist the desire to sin. So sinning became natural, even to the point that you did not know you had sinned since you no longer had a spiritual guide built inside you to tell you the difference (such as the fellow in Romans chapter 7, *long story another rabbit trail*). Without immediate or quick punishment humanity seemed to be getting by with sin.

I know that some *good* teachers out there (teachers that I learn from) do not believe that there was an actual snake talking to Eve in the garden. They believe that it was a metaphor. For now, I am going to go with it as a literal snake. You have to have a body to have rights (i. e. dominion) on earth. God set it up that way. It seems that the serpent had to loan its body to satan so he could approach Eve in subtlety. In his natural state, satan was a stronger and more powerful being than Adam in his *flesh alone.* However, with the backing of God on the side of humanity, satan was nothing. If it were not because of the set order of God that blanketed all dimensions, then satan could have come to earth and forced humanity to be subject to him; basically, spiritual slavery and spiritual rape. If satan could force you or kill you, he would have done so already, so do not fear him. Adam had the complete backing of the power of God but did not use it. Words spoken by Adam had authority from someone more powerful than satan, but Adam did not use what was at his fingertips (or at the tip of his tongue, I should say) because his arrogant soul thought he could handle it on his own. God allowed free will, not slavery. Adam had to choose to yield to satan, thereby enslaving us all. The subtlety of the snake which satan used, which had certain rights as a critter of earth's population, gained him the time he needed to get Adam to listen (*yes, I think we could*

68

talk to critters back then, our creation was very exalted compared to where we have fallen). Adam should have kicked the serpent out once he realized the serpent's words were in contradiction to the words of God. We know what happened— Adam did not use his authority, and God allowed this for He had given the earth to man.

God would not allow satan to invade and force humanity the same way He Himself did not invade and force His fix to things. In addition, as I said before, God had already looked into all the future paths that humanity had before them and knew that man was going to choose a path that led to hell. I am sure Adam thought he was "trying" this out and thinking he could come back to where he was if he did not like "death" since he did not know (have experience with) what "death" meant. Adam thought like many of our teenagers think today; "It will not happen to me", "I will find my way back", or "I can handle it." That may work in the physical world but in the spiritual realm you are either perfect or you do not qualify. You cannot stray, indulge your flesh and soul in vanity, and then return unstained. God said He did not want us to "know" evil. The "know" there is to be intimate with, to get naked with, expose ourselves to, or exchange in intercourse with evil. This "know" is like Adam "knew" Eve and she became pregnant. This did not happen by them shaking hands and talking over coffee.

Once humanity was dead spiritually, satan did not have to "tempt them" any longer to sin, because from the wrong tree forward, humanity would be born sinful. Disconnected from life, they were by default, connected to death—and death is to steal, kill, destroy, and lie. Once born, a human only had to breathe and their now selfish nature of death would have the baby self-absorbed. In short, we lust and envy by nature because we are born separated from the kind of life that does not lust and envy. Until a human showed up that could overrule the dead nature within, what could those in Adam do? During the 4000 years of satan's uninterrupted rule, the soul of man could override his spiritually dead nature and not commit *that* particular sin *that* particular time. Nevertheless, all the strength and effort of a righteous living man could not override the fact that he still wanted to satisfy self, to lust, and envy. Therefore, the very fact that he *wanted* and

Jeremiah C. Southerman

desired to look at the beautiful young woman makes him a sinner, even if he never looks and lust. For an example of this, read the book of Job. I will shorten the book considerably for you to make my point, but go read it to get a fuller image. We see that God calls Job "an upright man"- **And the LORD said unto Satan, Hast thou considered my servant Job, that *there is* none like him in the earth, a perfect and an upright man, one that feareth God, and escheweth evil? (Job 1:8).** One of the reasons Job had such good things said about him by God was this- **I** (Job) **made a covenant with mine eyes; why then should I think upon a maid? (Job 31:1)** However, Job also knew that he needed a redeemer- **For I know *that* my redeemer liveth, and *that* he shall stand at the latter *day* upon the earth (Job 19:25).** Therefore, he was a sinner by nature, just one that had extremely good judgment and a strong will to fight our natural tendencies toward sin. However, by the fact that he had the desire to sin, meant he needed redeemed. Job fought this temptation by the power of his soul. If he would have followed what was natural for him, his death nature would do what satan's normal desire would have him do, which would be to lust after the young woman.

When we make a mistake on a test, we would love to rip the test up and start over fresh. Many of us would do the same thing with our lives at times because of the mistakes we have made, if we could. However, to do this, a person must be born anew and start from the beginning, again. God makes a way for this to happen in the spirit realm; that is where the term "born-again Christian" comes from. It happens in your human spirit, which is the parent force behind and beyond the soul and body that we can contact with our five senses naturally. Again, men of honor from the Old Testament, such as Enoch, Job, Joseph, Samuel, and others, overrode sinful actions with strong will power, but they could not change their nature that still wanted to sin- **Can the Ethiopian change his skin, or the leopard his spots? *Then* may ye also do good, that are accustomed to do evil (Jer. 13:23).** The answer is, "No!" We are born into a fallen world that makes it normal, or makes us accustomed, to doing "evil" as defined by God. We cannot change the nature of our parent force (i. e. the spirit that is out of our reach) unless we are "born again" which takes someone "over there" in the spirit realm to do that for us. Praise the Lord! He has made

How God Got Mary Pregnant

a way! As I said above, Job made a covenant with his soul (think of it as logic vs. emotion) to not look upon a young woman with lust in his heart. He was applying logic for he had the knowledge that he could not control the temptation if he allowed the temptation. Just like intelligent people today would like to be high on drugs to forget about the stresses of life for a while, but do not because they also know that to embrace such activities is dangerous, risky, and leads to no good. Instead they learn to control, restrain, and manage their stress by overriding emotion with logic. This can be accomplished well by applying Philippians 4:8 to our lives. (*I'm not telling you.....go read it*)

We see in scripture that man's best was far short of God's minimum, such as- **But we are all as an unclean *thing*, and all our righteousness *are* as filthy rags;** that is talking about a woman's used monthly menstrual cycle cloth/i. e. "rag". Imagine grabbing a tool of some kind (*because we don't want to touch it either*) and holding that thing up to God and saying, "I present my good works for your inspection God"...*repulsive huh?-***and we all do fade as a leaf; and our iniquities, like the wind, have taken us away (Isa. 64:6).** This is because God is a Spirit, but our fallen flesh by nature dominates us, which makes us view things from lowly thoughts. While He maintains His Spiritual point of view on high, which He gave us access to by His work in our domain. If it were not for Jesus coming to our domain in flesh to retake that domain then none would have a chance to escape this walking death (think of this life like animation). It takes perfection to enter heaven because it is a perfect place. Since we were not perfect the only hope we had was for a perfect human (because God had given humans the authority here) to come along that was not from Adam's genealogy, but still wearing a "body of Adam,"— just not housing a spirit from Adam — that could dethrone satan. With this, He gives us His score on judgment day, since we all have to stand before the throne of judgment of the One who put us on this earth to begin with. Praise Jesus! He did just that! However, He had to do it a certain way— the same way mechanics build and rebuild our contraptions; they must do it in certain ways. This is where most religious-minded folks (who do not study what the Bible *really* teaches) fall into dispute with me. In other words, people who have partial imagery, yet are convinced they have all knowledge, cannot learn

Jeremiah C. Southerman

since they already know it all. They are comfortable with their doctrinal position (*the old "comfort zone" thing*). As long as their position is not against God or His plan, and it does not erode the foundation, which is Jesus Christ and Him crucified, then they are not in any danger of going to hell. One such doctrine they feel comfortable with says: "God is sovereign and in total control". God has a degree of sovereignty, but it is unlike they teach because He is NOT in TOTAL control. When one evaluates the "God's sovereign" doctrine it violates total imagery from the Bible. For if God did not value the free will of man above His own will, then He would not have created us to begin with since He knew we were going to sin before He created us. Okay,............... some of you religious people .... Think.................... I know it is hard for some of you, but try really hard on this one to *think* instead of feel............... (Thinking? that means to reason this out). Do not "emote" on this one, okay, are you ready?.............. here we go read slow now ......where,..... sin,.......is.......... God,.......is,...... NOT,.......in,.........control I know when you are brainwashed to believe otherwise that is hard to conceive of. I know that because I was brainwashed myself. If He were sovereign, then His will would be done on earth as it is in heaven. Furthermore, Jesus would not have wasted His breath by praying such a prayer in Luke 11:2. Free will means just that; FREE WILL. This means if Adam and Eve had decided NOT to have children, God would have lost all but those two at that point. God was not going to force Adam to rape Eve, hypnotize, or drug them into having sex. But in His wisdom to get the children He wanted He made sex sooooo powerful. It was by the free-will choice of the first two humans and they had the free will to go either way on that. However, sex is strong and God knew what He was doing long before He made it. You MUST consider that scenario in the acquisition of knowledge and plug that fact into total imagery as you study and embrace or reject doctrine. Otherwise, throw out free will! However, if you do that, then just throw out the Bible, which makes you just like the world, which makes satan happier. When God placed Adam in authority over creation, this man was God's son— a being, whom God loved more than he loved Himself. In doing so, creation was temporarily out of God's sovereign control. God had to honor man's decisions as long as a human was alive, because He had given Adam and Adam's offspring (*that's us*) that authority and would not take it away while

How God Got Mary Pregnant

He (God) was still in His Spiritual (non-physical) state. Part of His job in becoming a physical human was so that He could "legally" (since humans have the legal right on earth) take back control of humanity's domain. God's temporary lack of complete sovereignty on earth is why He had to do things a certain way. I am not teaching that God is our equal and He cannot act on earth without "permission", however.

I will give a quick example of God "sneaking" His sovereign wisdom in, repeating again the spiritual story of what Jesus has done for us. God used the life of Barabbas as a teaching tool. He was the man the Jews asked of Pilate to be set free at Jesus trial. Barabbas was (*and this is important to note*) a *rebel* who was being held in *bondage* for "*murder and robbery*". The Bible does not come right out and say he did either of these two crimes but he is associated with those that did, and he was a *rebel*. In texts older than the King James Version, Barabbas' first name is recorded, as being "*Jesus*". Way back this fellow named Origen (a church father) was transcribing the Bible and omitted the first name of Barabbas in reverence to Jesus *the Christ*. This is a good example of an ignorant, carnal mind that wanted to do a "good work" for God (*with a good intention, I point out*) but his carnal good-intending mind got in the way of that which is spiritual. What Origen did was rob us (future believers) of spiritual insight. God is wise and inserts the story repeatedly so we can "see" it better. Origen broke a spiritual rule set in place by God (Rev. 22:19.) In Origen's mind he wanted to show respect to Jesus by not having His name associated with a criminal. I do believe Origen's heart was right but his choice was wrong (much like many doctrines we cling to today). What did Origen rob from us? In the Aramaic language "Bar" means "son of". Example: in **Mat 16:17- And Jesus answered and said unto him, Blessed art thou, Simon Barjona:** Jesus was saying to Simon, blessed art thou Simon, *son of Jona*. In Greek the name is run together: "Barjona". The word "abba" means "father" so "bar-abba" is, "son of the father". Thus this rebellious person, Barabbas, who was associated with murder and thievery whose name was, in Greek: "Jesus Barabbas", and in Aramaic: "Jesus bar Abba" and in the fullest tense, "Jesus the son of the father". He was set free, while "Jesus the son of The Father" went to the tree (Galatians 3:13). This Barabbas chap was just another type and shadow of a bigger spiritual lesson, which is: God only had two sons. One was Adam, who became a *rebel* against God and introduced *murder* and *robbery*

73

Jeremiah C. Southerman

and put in place the *bondage* Jesus (the last Adam) bought us out of and all the sin we see in the earth. Adam is not recorded to have robbed or killed anyone, in a fleshly manner, that is. However, he was a rebel and he did kill us all spiritually and robbed us all of what God had in store for His kids. In Adam's rejection of God, Adam made satan his father. Here in **John 8:44** we see God's attitude towards the ways of men: **Ye are of your father the devil, and the lusts of your father ye will do. He was a murderer from the beginning, and abode not in the truth, because there is no truth in him. When he speaketh a lie, he speaketh of his own: for he is a liar, and the father of it.** Imagery here is that the physical offspring of Adam, "Adamites" (*that's us humans*), the sons and daughters of our dead spiritual father satan, due to our spiritually dead birth, (from our mothers womb) were set free if we choose it, while Jesus, the Son of His living Spiritual Father took our place in death … I will say that slightly different because it may help some. Adam (jesus) the first son of the Father, created from dirt 6000 years ago, rebelled against his Father God. In doing so became a spiritual murderer of all humanity, a thief, and by default, made satan his father, who did not want him as a son. But this Adam and all that are in him (us from natural birth) was set free from the bondage sin imposed upon him/us by the grace of this last Adam (Jesus), Son of The Father, created in Mary's womb 2000 years ago, who took Adam's death penalty for him at the hands of the Roman Government. That is God subtlety sneaking sovereignty into the happenings of men well in advance to get a man that He (God) knew was going to be a thug, into the right place at the right time so that he (Barabbas) could help teach us (you and me) the gospel. In an individual's life, God is sovereign when He gets permission from each of us. In humanity as a whole, God is sovereign when He can work it in, as in the example of Barabbas. To say God is in charge of all things (i. e. all sovereign) is simply wrong doctrine. The residue that doctrine leaves in the back of our mind is, "if God is sovereign then God is a loser. I just as well do all I can to enjoy my fleshly life, collect toys till I die and then see what happens" sounds like a satanically inspired twisted doctrine to me.

God does usually work through a human, or a human has to ask God in prayer to intervene in what is going on around that person's life here on earth. All it takes is one human to give God what He needs to act. There are times we see God's hand and are not told from the Bible

How God Got Mary Pregnant

if a human asked God to get involved (such as when worms ate king Herod, the confusion of languages at the tower of Babel, and the flood of Noah's time). We see many places in the Bible where God does act in the affairs of men to bring about what is best for men, which is the spiritual destination of being back with Him, just as He and Adam discussed (again, the example of the "near kinsman", in Ruth 3:12-13 and chapter 4). God involves Himself little in the physical affairs of men but will get involved to steer us back towards Him. For example, God loves freedom, so He would rather see humans have freedom to live our lives to the fullest. He would rather see us operate in free societies, not communism. However, He will allow us to set up our own governments, stupid or free as they may be. His gospel will get you saved in any government. We see satanically influenced governments try to make the Bible illegal. In addition, we see satanically inspired people work against Biblical life-styles as often as they can. Normally, we see God working in conjunction with someone. He has a plan for humanity; that plan is the Gospel message of Christendom. He has had to manipulate humanity onto a safer path that kept us alive until the Redeemer could get here. We are like lost sheep, and gullible children headed for destruction. Manipulation differs from being forced; manipulation does not violate our free-will. To say that God is absolute sovereign is to say man has no free will, which is foolish since there is sin and death all around, which obviously, is not God's will.

Keep in mind the only two people that really understood how "dead" they were was Adam and Eve. They are the only two that were able to compare their later fallen condition with their perfect past condition. Without the benefit of this comparison that those two had, everyone else tends to think we can work things out if we could just get rid of the opposition. We think that would bring us peace. Many times that actually means to "kill" that man in opposition. Look at the Middle East. They are trying to fix things by killing each other off. With that mindset (and we all are born with it), that makes God Himself in opposition! God could not just step in and take control because that would violate the dominion God gave man in running the affairs of men. If God could "fix" things, it would be His way (the right way), but fallen man, who is in charge and has the right to rule the kingdoms of men, would object to God's ways because our minds think in carnal, physical, and earthly terms. The Bible says- **Because the carnal mind *is* enmity against God: for it is not subject to the law of God, neither indeed can be (Romans 8:7).** History shows that ideas like hitler and stalin had, do not work. Even well meaning leaders, like the founding fathers of the U.S.A. had ideas that only worked when the voter had a moral conscience. Otherwise, as we see today, the system falls apart- **There is a way that seemeth right unto a man, but the end thereof *are* the ways of death (Prov. 16:25).** God would be an alien invader if He did anything without the cooperation of a man. Since He follows His own rules, He needed cooperation from a human. When we read the way God created everything, we see that He spoke things into existence. Before humanity, that was the job of the Godhead Being called the Word, which Mary later gave birth to (we can read how He spoke things into being in the creation account in Gen 1 and 2). Once humanity was here, their right to choose had to come into the equation. Therefore, the best thing for God to do is get Himself into the earth as a man, with flesh and blood, to save humanity from the eternal damnation.

Humanity, being spiritually dead and cut off from true intelligentsia, needed help. Since Adam chose to decide for himself (and in turn, passed that to you and me) what was intelligent and what was not, he limited our access to knowledge. Both our enemy, satan, and our best friend, God, live in a spirit realm where we fight our biggest battles. God tells us- **For we wrestle not against flesh and blood, but against principalities, against powers, against the rulers of the darkness of this world, against spiritual wickedness in high *places* (Eph. 6:12).** In short, we fight against spirit beings for control of our thoughts. The battle *is in* our minds and *for our* minds. That is why the human agents of our enemy, who also have the authority to act within the kingdoms of men, work so hard to pervert the minds of our youth. We need help in this battle. However, in our blindness to the fact that we are born with satan's arrogant, prideful, and self-centered nature, we think we can handle things, but only the end is destruction. Read Proverbs 16:25 again- **There is a way that seemeth right unto a man, but the end thereof *are* the ways of death.** It is a simple fact fellow humans, our intellect will not get us out of this, for the problem is spiritual at its core.

SO WHAT IS GOD DOING ABOUT IT?

On with the saga. All things within the kingdoms of men are now corrupt. Even the very atoms Adam was made from and the air he breathes. All things carnal are unacceptable to God's kingdom and the only way in is to be made perfect. His only way to make us perfect is to get Himself into our kingdom, however, now that He has turned earth over to humanity. His only legal way into the earth is through a mother's womb- **Jesus answered, "Verily, verily, I say unto thee, Except a man be born of water and *of* the Spirit, he cannot enter into the kingdom of God" (John 3:5).** In that verse, the "water" is amniotic fluid (i. e. natural birth). What He is saying is that,#1) only a human "born of water" or natural birth, via a womb of a woman can enter the kingdom of God. And,#2) the human who was born of a natural mother on earth must then later be "born-again" (that is the born "of the Spirit" part of the verse above) at some point in their natural life. Then and only then, can they enter into heaven. Regardless of how many good, wonderful deeds you do, they will NOT get your dead spirit past the barrier or "through the pearly gates", as many people say. Being born of water is your legal right into the earth. That is why satan has no rights of his own and uses people to gain access to — and work through — God's creation (satan used a snake the first time). Now there are willing men and women working for him. Since Adam passed on a corrupted body to you, your body cannot enter the spiritual kingdom where God dwells, but your spirit can if it came from God. However, until you are born again, your spirit came from Grandpa Adam. If you have done the Romans 10:9-10 confession (*lookie there, I called it a "confession", not a "thing"*), then your spirit is born again and came from heaven. It is not from earth or from Adam as it used to be and as your flesh still is. Your spirit lives inside of corrupt flesh and both your flesh and spirit interact with your soul. Your soul does not regard God or man, it only judges the evidence presented, as a judge in a courtroom. It is our job to present more truthful evidence to our soul — to present what God says is true in His Holy Bible. This truth is contrary to what the fallen, decaying, physical world (built mostly by satan's influence) says to our five senses. It is possible to retrain, or renew, our soul. Paul tells the Christians- **For which cause we faint not; but though our outward man** (our bodies) **perish, yet the inward *man*** (our soul) **is renewed day by day (II Cor. 4:16).** We do that by washing it with the Word, the Bible. Our flesh, being corrupt, will not be glorified as Jesus' was. His flesh owned no sin so God glorified that same flesh, though it came from Adam, but it belonged to Jesus. It had no sin because He used the power of the living spirit within Him to beat that Adamic thing back all day, every day. He purged His own Adamic flesh in His death. In our case, we get completely new bodies. God wants this for all of us, for God is love and wants no one to perish- **The Lord is not slack concerning his promise, as some men count slackness; but is longsuffering to us-ward, not willing that any should perish, but that all should come to repentance (II Peter 3:9).**

As soon as man sinned, God initiated the plan. He began early to have men *speak* a prophecy of the coming Seed- **And the LORD God said unto the serpent, Because thou hast done this, thou *art* cursed above all cattle, and above every beast of the field; upon thy belly shalt thou go, and dust shalt thou eat all the days of thy life: And I will put enmity between thee and the woman, and between thy seed and her seed; it shall bruise thy head, and thou shalt bruise his heel" (Gen. 3:14-15).** Note that God says *it* (salvation) will be the seed of the woman;

How God Got Mary Pregnant

Jesus (the Seed) does not count His genealogy back to Adam because God is His father, and Adam is His half brother. He is half brother because Jesus would get His body from Adam via Mary but His spirit (the parent force) would come from God.

When satan told God he had gotten himself a kingdom and God had lost His, God probably told satan, "No you pitiful idiot, you only think you got a kingdom. I knew this was going to happen even before I created you and I have already made provision for my children and to use you in my ultimate plan, before I destroy you forever in the lake of fire." The method God used was the same method He used to create nearly everything else; words (mankind was the exception). He began speaking of His own coming and that *was* the gospel at that time. Peter tells us that Noah was a preacher of righteousness- **And spared not the old world, but saved Noah the eighth *person*, a preacher of righteousness, bringing in the flood upon the world of the ungodly (II Peter 2:5).** Noah was preaching *that* particular message. Think about it; there was no law, no ten commandments, and no set of rules written down as a standard, and no denominations of men to adhere to. Remember, there were no Old or New Testament to instruct humanity at this time. Therefore, Noah could not hold over them the sin of breaking "the law"- **Wherefore, as by one man sin entered into the world, and death by sin; and so death passed upon all men, for that all have sinned: For until the law sin was in the world: but sin is not imputed when there is no law. (Rom. 5:12)** So, if there is no law or if sin is not defined, how do you know if you are sinning? If sin had no identifiers then how could God point a finger at anyone and say they sinned? **Nevertheless, death reigned from Adam to Moses, even over them that had not sinned after the similitude of Adam's transgression, who is the figure of him that was to come (Rom 5:12-14).** "After the similitude of Adam" means, "sinned on purpose". Paul's point here in Romans was that we are by *nature* sinners, because our spirit is dead. If you put someone in a room with no windows the moment they were born, slid them food under the door, and they lived and died there never making contact with any other human, not having anything to do with our fallen society (they would never lust, steal, kill, cheat, lie and so on), they would still die a sinner because their spirit was never born again via belief in the gospel about Jesus. Noah's message about a coming judgment and the only escape was to be IN the ark was the message, which they did not believe. *For us today Jesus is that ark.*

Humanity as a whole group could not understand it was wrong to be as they were. God had to work through sneaky means. Another example of this is the "words" that spell out a prophecy about the coming Messiah in the names God inspired the line of Seth to name their sons. I am sure men had no idea they were proclaiming a prophecy by naming their sons. However, when one strings together the names from Adam to Noah you get a prophetic sentence. The same "prophetic naming" begins again after the flood with the patriarchs, kings, and prophets of Israel. This actually continues to be a prophetic tool that continued for 4000 years until the promised words became flesh (Jesus). All of this is an interesting study on its own, and I would suggest researching it on your own. Someone has a video about this subject on youtube.com (here is the link) https://www.youtube.com/watch?v=fAHR7xroIIQ.

For now, here are the names from Adam to Noah, and their meanings:

Name	Means
1. Adam	man
2. Seth	appointed
3. Enos	misery and mortal
4. Cainan	sorrow
5. Mahalaleel	the blessed one
6. Jared	shall come down
7. Enoch	teaching
8. Methuselah	His death shall bring
9. Lamech	despairing
10. Noah	peace/comfort

The names put together as a sentence reads, *"Man-appointed-misery and mortal-sorrow;-the blessed one-shall come down-teaching.-His death shall bring-despairing-peace and comfort."* Note that God is using words spoken

How God Got Mary Pregnant

by *men* to "create" something in a realm that He no longer has absolute authority to control without cooperation of man. Remember, as long as there was no Adam to hand dominion over to, God was in sovereign control and God spoke what HE wanted. The Lord takes the following position- **The heaven, *even* the heavens, *is* the LORD'S: but the earth hath he given to the children of men (Psalms 115:16).** As soon as He turned it over to His son, Adam, God no longer had dominion, Adam did. If any of you are choking because of me calling Adam God's "son", go read Luke chapter 3. If you are in a hurry, here is the last verse- **Which was *the son* of Enos, which was *the son* of Seth, which was *the son* of Adam, which was *the son* of God (Luke 3:38).** *If you remove the King James italics, on this one, it reads the same.*

God used words to create all things when He was in charge. He is the same God always, because He never changes- **Jesus Christ the same yesterday, today and forever (Hebrews 13:8).** He also tells us that in the Old Testament- **For I *am* the LORD, I change not; therefore, ye sons of Jacob are not consumed (Mal. 3:6).** If your church has any silly doctrine that teaches God is different in anyway and does things differently today than He did at any point in human history, find another church! He is no respecter of persons, so anything that worked for one human will work for any human. He made us all in His image—in His likeness — and we are all to speak like Him and speak what He speaks. I want to look at some verses that give us an insight into how words are "handled" in the spirit realm. Note the imagery here in Revelation as if the prayers of the saints are more than just words. They are *things* with sustenance that carry weight that can be picked up, moved, put in a bowl or tracked as they pass through the air and/or dimensions- **Revelation 5:8-And when he had taken the book, the four beasts and four *and* twenty elders fell down before the Lamb, having every one of them harps, and golden vials full of odours, which are the prayers of saints.** The word "odours" does not mean "smell" as in *the smell* that is in the air, like our English word "odor", but rather, something that *makes* a smell. We smell the odor of freshly baked bread. The smell is in the air, the bread is the source of the smell. Bread is a tangible thing; smell is not. The odor talked about here is similar to that scenario. It is a powder, incense; a tangible thing that can be pinched and thrown into a fire that creates a sweet odor. In the Strong's concordance, again, *thumiama (thoo-mee'-am-ah)* from G2370; an *aroma*, that is, fragrant *powder* burnt in religious service; by implication the *burning* itself:- incense, odour. If our prayers were only sweet odors in the air, they could not "fill up" vials. In order "to fill up" a vial, it must be a tangible substance. Something must be "something" (i. e. have mass) if substance is transferred into the vial- **Revelation 8:3-And another angel came and stood at the altar, having a golden censer; and there was given unto him much incense, that he should offer *it* with the prayers of all saints upon the golden altar which was before the throne.** Here we see an angel about to offer incense with the prayers. If prayers are only words that vibrate the air then they are only real within the atmosphere as long as there are listening devices, such as ears or machines. However, in scripture we see that our words pass into the higher dimensions where they are collected, placed in a container, and offered up to God- **Revelation 8:4-And the smoke of the incense, *which came* with the prayers of the saints, ascended up before God out of the angel's hand.**

It would seem, then, from these three verses in Revelation, that as our prayers "rise up" to God they are accompanied by a sweet, pleasing odor (maybe *aroma* sounds better to our modern ears), indicating that God loves it when He receives our prayers. In other places in the Bible, such as Amos 7:9-17- God is instructing Amos to "speak" words (i. e. prophesy) about the things coming on the land. He also tells Amos that the land "is not able to bear all his words given". The imagery here is of an overloaded truck, or something that is overwhelmed by the volume of the mass imposed upon it. Words carry *weight*; we are just naturally blind to it. Also, in Hosea 1:4-11 God tells Hosea to name his kids certain names that symbolize in prophetic ways what God will bring upon Israel for their disobedience to Him. This is similar to the method He used when He had Adam name Seth and Seth name Enos, and so on. Words in the spiritual realm, it seems, are something more than *just* a means to communicate.

ABRAHAM

After proclaiming Jesus' coming for about 2000 years, God's next step was to channel that coming into a family line. Beginning with Abraham, He did just that. Here is the way that came about. God operates by faith- **But without faith *it is* impossible to please *him* for he that cometh to God must believe that he is and *that* he is a rewarded of them that diligently see him (Hebrews 11:6).** God needed someone with faith on the earth to help Him further the plan of salvation. He found that faith in Abram. God found issues they both related to well; they neither had kids at the time, and both wanted kids and had much to offer children. In Abraham's life, we find many of God's principles put into action. First, Abraham had simple faith. He believed it because God said it. Then he followed up his belief with action. An example of that is- **Now the LORD had said unto Abram, Get thee out of thy country, and from thy kindred, and from thy father's house, unto a land that I will shew thee (Gen. 12:1).** In verse four, we see that "**Abram departed**".

God made a deal with Abram. His deal went like this: "Abram if you will follow me and obey me, I will be your God and I will be a blessing to you, and you will be a blessing to all the earth through the kids you do not yet have. I will make your grandkids like the stars of the night sky and

83

Jeremiah C. Southerman

like the sand on the seashore". Abraham is the father of the Israelites, and the father of the Jews (which is the last remaining tribe of ancient Israel). Moreover, we as Christians today are grafted into his family line (Gal. 3:7). Also, note in the verses that his name is Abram, not Abraham, as we know him today. This also is a lesson in words creating, manipulating, or changing the future. God changed Abram's name- **Neither shall thy name any more be called Abram, but thy name shall be Abraham; for a father of many nations have I made thee (Gen. 17:5).** God changed his name so that each time he said "my name is Abraham" he would prophecy, or declare, that he was the "father of a multitude". God did this because words create and He made man lower than Himself, but like Himself. He creates out of nothing using words and we have the ability to manipulate what He has already created by using words. His blessing is on this method. He had man speak things He knew man needed without having to explain to men what He was doing. Our minds struggle with the concept of getting our building material from "nothing"—as we count stuff, but all things are possible with God. Faith is the building material (substance) in the spirit realm and faith is all you need. God was manipulating the domain of humanity with words spoken by them to accomplish His will for the good of all. Too many of us speak of things we feel (emotion) or think (human reasoning) in our negative, fallen souls. In doing so, we are speaking death to our future, for our soul gets its information from a fallen, dying, decaying, physical world. On the other hand, if you pour the Holy Bible into you faithfully, the lies of the fallen, satanically inspired world around us will begin to lose their power over the way we think, because our soul will be getting information/evidence from another source.

Now back to God's deal with Abraham. By using Abraham's faith, God was able to prepare the lineage of Judah for Jesus to come to earth through. And it was words exchanged by two beings, one a God and one a man, that gave Jehovah God the right to then cut a covenant in front of Abraham (as a man, Abraham needed something to see, to record for us today). The smoking furnace and burning lamp was actually cutting a covenant at that same time, between themselves- **And it came to pass, that, when the sun went down, and it was dark, behold a smoking furnace, and a burning lamp that passed between those pieces** (of

84

How God Got Mary Pregnant

the sacrificial offering) (**Gen. 15:17**). The smoking furnace and burning lamp represented God Jehovah and God the Word, who when the physical time to fulfill the covenant came, would be God the Father and Jesus the Son (go read the account in Gen. Chapter 15). This covenant is forever binding. Abraham was familiar with blood covenants; he knew that a blood covenant meant it was unbreakable. Or rather, only by death can a blood covenant be fulfilled. Jehovah was cutting this covenant with the Word as one of Abraham's <u>descendants</u>, but not only for Abraham but also all of his unborn descendants. Therefore, for it to be annulled or fulfilled, meant either God, or all of the children promised to Abraham through Isaac, would have to die. Is it not interesting how the Jews have been under attack since the time satan discovered the seed would be coming through the tribe of Judah? Try as he did, satan never succeeded in killing the Jews. Jesus did however fulfill the blood covenant by shedding His. God gave Abraham a vision of the long-term future of his kids. A horror fell on Abraham when he saw many of the things his kids would go through in the thousands of years to come, but also a joy when he saw the Savior come through them. That is how Jesus could say to the Jews in His day- **Your father Abraham rejoiced to see my day: and he saw** *it,* **and was glad (John 8:56).**

God was having Abraham speak his own future that both he and God wanted for him. In that future would be Mary, through whom God, naming himself Jesus, would get into the earth. Jesus came from a mother and that is the only legal entry into the earth- **Verily, verily, I say unto you, He** (satan) **that entereth not by the door** (a mother's womb) **into the sheepfold** (humanity), **but climbeth up some other way** (in the body of a snake), **the same is a thief and a robber. But he** (Jesus) **that entereth in by the door** (Mary's womb) **is the shepherd of the sheep (John 10:1-2).** No human mother, no legal entry. So satan is not legal, and his voice (which speaks his words, i. e. lies) has no authority. Yet, satan gets all kinds of power, borrowed or stolen from us, from *our belief* in his lies. We have the authority to act and speak since we are human. If we act and speak what satan wants us to, then he, not God, gets his way. Neither God nor satan has that authority; they both had to borrow it from someone—some to "do good" (God's will) and some to "do evil" (satan's will).

Now back to Abraham and the covenant cut with God. In Matthew we find the genealogy is of Joseph's side of the family- **The book of the generation of Jesus Christ, the son of David, the son of Abraham. Abraham begat Isaac; and Isaac begat Jacob; and Jacob begat Judas and his brethren (Matthew 1:1-2).** Note that the genealogy starts with Abraham, not Adam. There is a reason for it. Abraham, it seems, is the first person to have enough faith for God to cut a deal with that would end in getting Himself into the earth so that He could save men from eternal spiritual death. That would make Abraham the starting point of the father's side for the "seed by faith", not by sperm. This was a starting point of the faith that would become Jesus who would save humanity.

It takes sperm to impregnate a woman but God had none. Sperm comes from a man; thereby, all sperm is contaminated. Faith is the *substance* of things "hoped for". It, faith, is a tangible thing in the spirit realm; much like cash is to us. We have substance in our hand and trade that substance for other things of substance that we need or want, such as; milk and bread, burritos and beer, cars and trucks, houses and land, and clothes and stereos. In the spirit realm, we exchange faith for the things we need or want, such as; a loved one saved, protection from enemies, direction in life's big choices, healing from sickness, and clarity of doctrine. We also can use faith to get milk and bread, burritos and beer, cars and trucks, houses, land, clothes, and stereos, but God has little concern about the latter things. He says to seek Him first and these things will be added to your life (Matt. 6:24-34). He says He clothes the lilies of the field and takes care of the birds and how much more important are we than birds (*read all of Matthew Chapter 10*).

Abraham's faith gave God something to work with to give him and Sarah kids. In the covenant, Abraham also gave God the right to look after, and chastise, his grandkids—the Israelite's—until the promised Seed could get to earth to accomplish the needed task of paying the blood price on humanity's head. God asked Abraham to do a weird thing, however. He asked him to sacrifice his only son. God went almost all the way with Abraham in the sacrificing of Isaac; all the way to the point Abraham was coming down with the knife. We know that Abraham was going to go

How God Got Mary Pregnant

through with it, for the Bible says- **By faith Abraham, when he was tried, offered up Isaac: and he** (Abraham) **that had received the promises** (from God concerning Isaac) **offered up his only begotten *son*,** (Isaac) **Of whom it was said,** (from God, to Abraham) **That in Isaac shall thy seed be called:** (and Abraham) **Accounting that God *was* able to raise *him*** (Isaac) **up, even from the dead; from whence also he** (Abraham) **received him** (Isaac) **in a figure (Heb 11:17-19).** This shows us that if Abraham "received him in a figure" Abraham had already made up his mind that he was going to kill Isaac and get Isaac back from the dead. Abraham, by faith, was willing to follow God's instructions not knowing the reason God would ask such a thing. Abraham did not have the rest of the story as we do today — he had to go on faith alone. Abraham knew that it was through Isaac that his grandkids, which were going to "number like the stars in the night sky", were going to come through. Since he knew Isaac did not have kids yet, he knew God would have to raise Isaac from the dead to make God's first promise happen. This is the only time God even hints at human sacrifice to Himself. The witch doctors that serve satan reach towards this murderous perversion as often as they can. Now, why would God ask such a thing from a man? I know two reasons. I am not saying this is exhaustive, but first, it was, as most people teach (correctly, I might add) that it was another form of teaching about what He was going to do for humanity—a prophecy about the Savior. We see that when Isaac asked Abraham, "Hey dad what about the lamb?" Abraham's prophetic reply: "God will provide *Himself* a lamb for the burnt offering" (Gen. 22:7-8). And secondly, here is the part that I have never heard taught anywhere, by anyone, that must be learned via imagery and the help of the Holy Ghost............... God was "extracting" Abraham's faith to raise a dead son; not just faith in general, but a specific faith for a specific task. It does seem that God did not look into the future for God says- **And he** (God) **said, Lay not thine hand upon the lad, neither do thou anything unto him: for now** (a present tense word) **I know that thou fearest God, seeing thou hast not withheld thy son, thine only *son* from me (Gen. 22:12).** I do not think the future was God's focus. What I am getting here is that faith is something God can "see", as in: faith is something to look at, to take a snapshot of, that way God can show you off like any proud parent or coach does. Saying, "look at my friend Abraham's faith, isn't that

87

Jeremiah C. Southerman

a lot of faith!" And that faith was not there to been seen in the levels God wanted and needed it to be until Abraham carried out this next request. *"Now"*, God said, but not before that event it seems, did God know if Abraham was going to back out or not, for it is a human choice to take the next blind step in faith that God has asked of us. When we do faith grows. It was growing in Abraham as each second passed. This seems to indicate that God does not just *automatically* know all future timelines (not that He could not — I think His abilities are that big). Nor do I think that God was doing this only to "test" Abraham, as simple/ignorant Bible teachers teach (*seems very cruel for a Loving God, just to test a mortal man*). God had His eyes/focus/attention on the faith that was being produced in Abraham. At the right moment, God would stop Abraham and extract the faith produced, which happened when Abraham was coming down with the knife. Looking further at the faith of Abraham from a New Testament point of view, let us do a read-through first- **Even so faith, if it hath not works, is dead, being alone. Yea, a man may say, Thou hast faith, and I have works: shew me thy faith without thy works, and I will shew thee my faith by my works. Thou believest that there is one God; thou doest well: the devils also believe, and tremble. But wilt thou know, O vain man, that faith without works is dead? Was not Abraham our father justified by works, when he had offered Isaac his son upon the altar? Seest thou how faith wrought with his works, and by works was faith made perfect? And the scripture was fulfilled which saith, Abraham believed God, and it was imputed unto him for righteousness: and he was called the Friend of God (James 2:17-23).**

Now, let us break it down:

James 2:17-Even so this thing called **faith, if it hath not works,** an action accompanying it, **is dead, being alone-** just a concept or a distant belief, (vs.18)-**Yea, a man may say** to his brother in the Lord that he goes to church with…**Thou hast faith, and I have** calloused hands, tired feet and sweat on my brow from my **works:** But I, James, the Apostle, say, **shew me thy faith without thy works, and** as an example **I will shew thee my** active **faith by my** active **works.** In addition, this will go on to explain that just believing that there is a God only means you have accepted a concept of a Deity. (vs. 19): **Thou believest that there is one God; thou doest well: the devils also believe, and tremble.** (vs. 20)-**But wilt thou know, O vain man, that faith without works** which are accompanying actions **is dead?** It is only empty words that soothe itching ears. But since I, James, am just a normal man standing before you today that you have no respect for, let me use a famous example that all of us Jews respect, our father Abraham… (vs. 21)-**Was not Abraham our father justified by works,** an act, or action that displayed his belief, showing that his faith was more than just an accepted concept **when he had offered Isaac his son upon the altar?** (vs. 22)-**Seest thou-**or do you understand **how** this thing called **faith wrought with** that is; accompanied, helped with, co-labored with, the action in **his** Abraham's **works, and by** the action of his **works was** Abraham's **faith made perfect?** Note the word "perfect". Why would Abraham need perfect faith if God were not going to have him kill Isaac? Abraham needed "perfect" faith to be used for the thing God needed that perfect faith for. Abraham's faith was strong but not perfect. Not until Abraham endured, acted on, and carried out this action, could God extract it as "perfect" faith. A specific faith, formed in an exact test and trial, so it would be tailor-made faith, perfect to raise a son from the dead, **(vs. 23)-And the scripture was fulfilled which saith, Abraham believed God, and it was imputed unto him for righteousness: and he was called the Friend of God.** God needed sure faith, full faith; the kind that was not complete in Abraham until Abraham started down with the knife. Then, and not until then, could God extract from the situation what He needed from within the kingdoms of men, so it could be released when His Son Jesus, the man, whose body was still within the kingdoms of men, in a borrowed tomb, was dead. God wanted the faith perfect—His kind of faith. Abraham's doubts and fears were purged millisecond by millisecond as he progressed on in this faith walk. Faith is substance; substance is something you can touch. Therefore, this "faith" substance was extracted from the situation with Abraham as it was perfected in Abraham. That action of coming down with the knife was a witness that his belief (faith) was complete. The faith that Abraham had in God to raise Isaac from the dead had been there for Isaac, but not needed. God's power had to flow through a man to work in the kingdoms of men. Once the faith

Jeremiah C. Southerman

was developed in Abraham (at the last moment, *call it the last trillionth of a second),* God stopped Abraham, "bottled" the substance, and held it unused for 2000 years (as we count time) until He needed it. Then He sent an angel that rolled away the stone, opened the bottle, and released the faith; faith that originated in a man, therefore it had the authority of a man, to work something within the kingdoms of men. It was the same faith that the power was flowing through from God to raise Jesus from the dead.

When Jesus was resurrected from the dead, God brought Him to heaven and glorified Him as He is today. Jesus got His actual blood from faith (*the blood type comes from the father*) and His actual body from Mary who came from Adam. All Adam's kids had "dead blood", or blood with no "God life" in it. God said the life is in the blood- **For the life of the flesh *is* in the blood: and I have given it to you upon the altar to make an atonement for your souls: for it *is* the blood *that* maketh an atonement for the soul (Lev. 17:11).** That is, that physical life is in the blood. In Jesus' physical life, His blood could not be from Adam because Adam's was tainted. His blood had to come from God. Since God has no blood to build in Mary's womb from sperm, He did it by faith, because faith was the substance of the child He hoped for, the evidence of the child not seen.

Via Abraham's covenant, God gained more rights in human affairs. At first, it was through the Israelite's; then later, an actual human body on earth, from the Israelite nation. Once He became human, born to the line of King David, He had the royal right to the throne of an actual kingdom of men. That gave Jesus a legal right to take control of His throne, though we do not see Him taking full control of His Kingdom yet, because the harvest is not yet "ripe". His kingdom is not of this fallen, physical realm- **Jesus answered, "My kingdom is not of this world: if my kingdom were of this world, then would my servants fight, that I should not be delivered to the Jews: but now is my kingdom not from hence" (John 18:36).** Again His subjects are the born-again believers all over the earth. He is not here bodily (He is in heaven) so He still has to work through human agents until He takes total control. That is what the church as a functioning body is supposed to be doing—His will on earth. *We* are His hands, *we* are His feet, *we* are His mouthpiece, and *He* is the head- **For the husband is the head of the wife, even as Christ is the head of the church: and he is the saviour of the body (Eph. 5:23).** For further description on this, read I Corinthians chapter 12. Therefore, we are supposed to be functioning as Christ in the earth; ....shame on us.

Back to our saga. Once the way was prepared for Him to step into humanity as a human for the first time 2000 years ago, Gabriel the archangel was sent to talk to the virgin Mary, and Mary said, "be it unto me" (see Luke 1:38). 4000 years of stage set-up was complete. Permission and co-operation was given by a human (Mary) for the Holy Ghost to take the spirit (small "s") of He who had been a Deity Spirit (capital "S"), the One who had been "The Word" for eternity past. To collect the 4000 years of prophetic words about His coming to add the spirit to the substance that faith is (which is invisible to us), and that spirit of "The Word" was added to the faith-filled words that had been spoken about His bodily coming for 4000 years and He, the Holy Ghost, makes a visit to Mary's womb. This was not a mere deposit in Mary's womb—it was an act of creation. For the one-third of the Godhead called "The Holy Ghost" had created the first creation in conjunction with the God Being called "The Word" (Logos, in Hebrews). When the Logos spoke the words "light be," the Holy Ghost moved into action to make it so, and the creation came into being. By Mary's day, the time had come for the "seed words" to be sown into the kingdoms of men so they could now manifest within the kingdoms of men. If it could have been just a deposit by an archangel, satan being an archangel himself would have tried to stop it as he did when Daniel prayed and satan withstood Gabriel 21 days (see Daniel chapter 10). In this case with Mary, all satan could do was sit back and cry when the flaming Sword he had last seen protecting *"the way* of the tree of life" in the garden of Eden (Gen 3:24- i. e. God Himself) came down to deliver the package. Jesus said I am *"The Way"* (John 14:6). Now the Holy Ghost was bringing *The Way* into Mary's womb. Nine months later, The Way/The Word, became flesh and dwelt among us so that we could behold His glory. This was the same glory that God had intended for all of us to have if Adam would have chosen the other tree.

Jeremiah C. Southerman

Have doubts? I ask you then, if God catches our prayers in golden bowls, that pretty much demands that in the spirit realm those prayers made of words must have substance or "mass" as discussed earlier. In **Rev. 5:8,** it says- **And when he had taken the book, the four beasts and four *and* twenty elders fell down before the Lamb, having every one of them harps, and <u>golden vials</u>** (note my emphasis) **full of odours, which are the prayers of saints.** Since the Bible reveals to us this is what happens with prayers, which consist of words, why do we doubt that the prophecies, which consist of words spoken throughout the centuries, could not be "deposited" in Mary's womb— *Mary's golden vial*— thereby impregnating her with Holy words. The Holy words spoken in a physical world, deposited in a physical womb would give physical substance to The Holy Word to make Him flesh for Mary to deliver into this physical world. Since God's method of making His son (small "s", i. e., Adam) into flesh was no longer by His own authority as it was before there was Adam on earth, then He needed Mary's womb to "create" the life of the next Son (capital "S") in the Adamic domain of earth in order to retake that domain. What a plan! Jesus said in the parable of the sower, Mark 4:13-20- especially verse 14- **"The sower soweth the word".** Note the imagery in that statement that "words" are "seeds". Jesus is The Word; the Bible is made of words. Jesus is "The Seed" promised to Eve and to Abraham. Therefore, this means that the Logos would come to men to have them speak or write what He said into the kingdoms of men. This was how He would sow the "word seeds" into Mary's womb since He had no "sperm seed" to plant there. It is kind of like fathering Himself, weird as that may sound to us (*brings to mind an old Ray Stevens song, "I'm my own Grandpa"*). Just because it does not normally "work that way" in our fallen, faithless, small-dimensional, and carnal society does not mean it does not work. All things are possible with God (Mark 10:27). The apostles understood this. They open most of the letters to the churches (what we call the "books" of the New Testament today) with a blessing spoken to the churches. They were putting into practice what they knew.

The Ransom

Now, "The Ransom", Jesus The Way, was on the earth and satan had a problem on his hands, and he knew it. This child born to Mary had a spiritual candle brightly burning that satan had not seen since he snuffed out the "light" of Adam and Eve (we get a glimpse of it in Mark 9:3). But now, Jesus the Christ, the long spoken of Messiah, the promised Seed, Savior of the world, redeemer of mankind, the Lamb of God, earth's only spiritual hero, our All in all, was here to make a way to light our candles. Just as one candle can be used to light another candle and pass that light on, satan now had an issue, for the human sacrifice he had demanded, thinking it could not happen, was here to happen, despite his best efforts to stop it. His only chance then would be to get Jesus to sin, or stop humanity from killing him (the plan Peter had for the Christ).

A quick recap: God creates with words. It was God "The Word" which spoke, and the words manifested as the universe that is our home (read the creation story in Genesis). He began speaking His coming into the realm of humanity as soon as humanity sinned (remember the list I gave you of the prophetic names of the men prior to the flood. Later, He found a man, Abraham, who believed Him enough to channel the words into a genealogy that He would make into a nation (the nation of Israel). That nation would have the only God-given religion on earth. He would cut a covenant with them at Mount Sinai, which added to the covenant He had already cut with their ancestor Abraham. This covenant religion, otherwise known as the Law of Moses or Judaism, would show the world His plan played out in the annual Feast days (Lev. 23). During the many years of Israel's history it would be words, Holy Words, spoken by The Word, The Logos of God, the very one that would become Jesus, to men and women willing to listen and record His words (that is what we call the "Old Testament" today). One of those men was Isaiah. In Isaiah 7:14 he puts forth a prophecy about Mary (but never mentions her by name) 700 years before she lived. This is one of many examples of how The Word was slowly speaking Himself into the earth a little at a time through the lips of men- **Wherefore when he cometh into the world, he saith, Sacrifice and offering thou wouldest not, but a body hast thou prepared me (Hebrews 10:5).** All this speaking was creating a "body" in a kingdom that He no longer had full rights to create in Himself, by the voice of men who had the rights, with their co-operation. He was doing it *through* men with His inspired words to them. Nine months later, the words implanted in Mary's womb manifested as a male child that the rest of us, besides just Mary, could contact. He would be alive spiritually and physically with the ability to live the law that the nation of Israel (or any other) never could. He was killed by the religious system of the day, which was the religious leaders of His own people, backed by the Roman government. Three days later, He was raised by faith that no man alive had; the faith for that exact purpose, that had been developed inside Abraham two thousand years earlier (as we humans reckon time) and used on resurrection Sunday morning. That faith coupled with His own words (or prophecies) about His resurrection, backed by the power of the Holy Ghost, which is the same Holy Ghost that does all the "works" of God, brought Him back to life again. In Matt 26:61 and John 2:19 where Jesus said, "I" will build the temple in three days, referring to the fact that He would build or raise up His own "temple", or His own body, in three days. That is a strange concept relative to our way of thinking. Remember, He is much higher than we are — our limited minds stop working far short of His abilities. Most folks believe (and there is nothing wrong with this belief) that God the Father raised Jesus from the dead, and that is true because the three of them are one. I say that is not *all* there is to it. I guess you could say I want to put forth the *how* He did it since this book is about the mechanics of these events. God the Father sitting in the third heaven did not have the right to say within the kingdoms of men, "Jesus, My Son come forth from the grave", as we see Jesus saying to Lazarus (John 11:43). I put forth this teaching, bold as it may seem to others, that Jesus did raise *Himself* from the dead by, you guessed it…by speaking words (i. e. prophesying) about His resurrection from the dead before He even entered time and space and continued to do so while He was here, also. The Bible teaches- **So shall my word be that goeth forth out of my mouth: it shall not return unto me void, but it shall accomplish that which I please, and it shall prosper *in the thing* whereto I sent it (Isa. 55:11). And- Then said the LORD unto me, Thou hast well seen: for I will hasten** (Hasten means to keep constant watch over) **my word to perform it (Jer. 1:12).**

So, when Jesus "The Word" spoke words about His own resurrection before His death, He was assuring that the words had a mission that needed

How God Got Mary Pregnant

fulfilled. Until they accomplished what they had been sent to accomplish, they would remain until every "jot and tittle" was fulfilled (Matt 5:18). The same Holy Spirit that did all the creating way back at creation still had power, but the Holy Spirit was alien to earth so He sitting in the third heaven did not have the authority to speak His Devine will. Only a human has the authority in the kingdoms of men, but we lack power. God has power but lacks full authority. Therefore, co-laboring works great. The authority came from Jesus, the man, that's why He had to become a man and step out of His Deity to do so. He did not qualify for the job title if He were not fully human. Since as a human He poured the scriptures unto His soul and poured His soul into His father, He had a relationship with God that we see as impossible for us (because we love our pet sins more than we love Him) So in that good relationship He knew what God wanted Him to speak and He knew that as a human He had the authority so in words spoken before His death, He was doing His part of the plan to assure that He would not stay dead. The power came from the Holy Ghost who IS God. Faith, that must be present within the kingdoms of men, to act within the kingdoms of men had to be from or "of" a man to have authority or "a legal right to operate" within the kingdoms of men. God, the alien to earth had already gotten co-operation from Abraham to act in his children's genealogy, which blesses all the kingdoms of men. Under extreme pressure, Abraham had developed that faith to raise his son that he sacrificed from the dead to fulfill the plan of God for his personal life. In that same plan, God would get Himself a family on earth. This required an exact faith for an exact purpose. Both God and Abraham wanted kids. Both had a vision for as many kids as the sand of the sea and both were going to have to give up the only kid they had at the time to gain the billions (*maybe trillions*) to come. Here in Psalms 119 we find a prayer of Jesus written by a prophetic psalmist. We see Jesus the man speaking these very things as He is talking to God His father. Let me say that differently; Psalm 119 is the very words that Jesus the man would be speaking to His Father God when He would become a human hundreds of years later. One needs to keep in mind that satan hounded Jesus every day, bombarding His mind with thoughts just as he does us, just hoping Jesus would "take" one of satan's thoughts and act on it (read Matthew chapter six). Jesus would not accept one of satan's thoughts, but Jesus as a human needed assurances, strengthening and all the things we need as humans. He just knew where the real source was — His Father, and the Holy scriptures.

95

Here in Psalms we have insight to Jesus' daily life as to where He got His assurances and strengthening- **Psalms 119:49- Remember the word** (the covenant you and I cut in Abraham's time, *that would be the smoking furnace and burning lamp*) **unto** (me Jesus) **thy servant, upon which thou** (Father, God) **hast caused me** (Jesus) **to hope. verse: 50- This** (knowledge and remembrance of that covenant) *is* **my comfort in my affliction:** (that I have while living in this junk-yard of an earth in the kingdoms of men, knowing I will be beaten to death for them that hate me and, at best, do not understand me). **for thy word** (*note that it says "word"*) **hath quickened me.** Quicken means "to make alive." So, what did, "for thy *word* hath quickened me" do? They made him alive. In the teaching I am putting forth, those words made Him alive two times. First, they were spoken for 4000 years and prepared Him a body to dwell in on earth. That gave Him physical life. In addition, they made Him alive the second time, as well, by bringing Him back from the dead. It was words coupled with faith spoken about His resurrection by men (including Himself) within the kingdoms of men that gave the Holy Spirit authority to operate- **Hear my voice according unto thy lovingkindness: O LORD, quicken me according to thy judgment (Psalms 119:149).** The faith to carry out the "quickening" was extracted from Abraham years before. So, how powerful are our words?

Satan Uses Words Also

Jesus said- **The thief cometh not, but for to steal, and to kill, and to destroy: I am come that they might have life, and that they might have** *it* **more abundantly (John 10:10).** We have discussed satan's music— words put to a tune— that destroy. He also owns most of the media (*most of it*) which he uses destructively against us. In addition, on the personal level, we cannot escape his influence by turning off the world, even though we should turn it off — at least to reduce his influence. He still has day and night to lie to our spirit-man, hoping to get our soul to act on one of his suggestions which will lead to more destruction. It is words used by both sides; the Kingdom of God to give, and the kingdom of satan to take. God is love; satan is evil. God gives; satan steals. Lies are satan's tool to manipulate us into believing things that destroy our lives. His lies generally *seem,* at a glance, to line up with what we observe in the natural world, and look how he has affected the world. His lies lead a group in 9-11-2001 to kill as many as they could in a suicide planned hijacking. So how powerful are words? I suggest watching Ben Stein's documentary, Expelled: No Intelligence Allowed, to show you a good snap-shot of how satan hates words of wisdom to be spoken and how he fights in any way he can, the speaking of good words. And he works hard through his followers to sow his words of destruction.

Today, Jesus gives us His status with God the Father. He has made us sons and daughters of God as He is, minus the Deity (*this is if you have done the Romans 10:9-10 thing*). What a plan! A plan satan could not figure out until he read it in the book as righteous men and women were writing it down. He could not stop it; he has tried many times, in many ways throughout history and is still trying today. Just look at the onslaught from the political left against anything Godly. By observation alone, a thinking person should realize that there is good and evil at work; and the very fact that Christianity as a religion is so under attack more than any other since it began would show that *it* is the one in the cross-hairs of evil's big guns. Many "stars" in our entertainment world of today have "made a pact with the devil" (their own words, not mine). The devil, who is the god of this world, controls much of its wealth and will reward "stars" with carnal success (i. e. fame and fortune) for using their talents to draw young people away from God. We know that satan owns it and that he is a counterfeiter and that just as God is "a rewarder of those that diligently seek Him" (Hebrews 11:6), so satan rewards those who serve him in his decaying kingdom. Jesus the man would not have been tempted when satan was telling him, "I can give you all the kingdoms if you bow down and worship me," if satan did not own them to give them to Jesus. Satan knew where Jesus was headed, i. e. "King of the earth", and the temptation he was presenting to Jesus was to shorten Jesus' trip and bypass Jesus' brutal path to the Kingship (satan was offering Jesus His best life now so to speak). If Jesus would have done so then He would be dead today and satan would still have his kingdom and we would all be doomed to hell. However, praise Jesus' name! He lives so that we can too!

OK, SO WHAT?

If you read a headline that says, "5 billion light-years out in space the planet xyz is about to collide with the planet br-548". That may be interesting for those who enjoy astrophysics and astronomy, but there is no practical application for your life. In other words, "who cares?" So it is with the information of how Mary got pregnant if you could not extract something more than "just interesting" out of it that can be applied to your life. If you have been paying attention you will have noticed the heavy emphasis on the speaking of our own words, that our spirit needs to be born again (*the Romans 10:9-10 thing*), I have explained what "born again" is, and the instructions that we are three-in-one like Him and our spirits should be in charge *if* they are born again. That would be getting the soul/servant off the horse and our born-into-royalty spirit-man on the horse, which is controlling our fleshly bodies while we pass through this world that Adam passed on to us. Therefore, we should try to emulate Jesus, since He as The Word spoke all things into being on this earth before He step out of Deity, He even inspired men of old the speak His own human body into the kingdoms of men in "seed" form to use while on this earth. Then, should we as emulators of Him, speak as He spoke. Since we are ignorant of what to speak and we are from fallen origins and birthed in vanity, trained in vanity to think in vanity, then when we speak *our* words, they

How God Got Mary Pregnant

will, by default, be self-centered words; words of vanity, not the words God would speak, if He were speaking to our situation for us. If we speak His words about our situation, then we are one-step closer to being just as He is. Therefore, whatever your problem is, chances are there are verses in the Bible that came from His lips about your mess. Get a concordance and find them. Write them down- **And thou shalt write them upon the posts of thy house, and on thy gates (Deut 6:9).** Carry them around with you- **Let not mercy and truth forsake thee: bind them about thy neck; write them upon the table of thine heart (Proverbs 3:3).** Again, He tells us- **Bind them upon thy fingers, write them upon the table of thine heart (Proverbs 7:3).** (*Some orthodox Jews do this, literally*). You do not have to, but you do need to read and speak them aloud, and stay at it until your "soulish" thinking lines up with what the Bible says about your situation, NOT what your five senses are telling you. That is giving your soul the evidence it needs to believe something besides circumstances, since your soul cares for neither God nor man, just evidence (see again Luke 18:1-8). It is *intoxicating* your soul with things that seem impossible normally. I will touch on what I mean briefly. It revolves around this verse: **Eph.-5:18- And be not drunk with wine, wherein is excess; but be filled with the Spirit.** If a small man, one about five and a half feet tall, 145 pounds when wet, were to walk into a bar and begin drinking to the point he was intoxicated. At that point, if someone was to challenge him to "whip" the big fellow at the other end of the bar who is about seven feet tall and 350 pounds, in his distorted state of mind, he might start thinking he could do this "seemingly impossible" task. All bets from other barroom patrons would be against the little man. In this case, I would bet against him also. However, this case does not include the spirit realm or the power of faith in what Gods words says. An example could be that you, a human, are feeling small in comparison to the cancer report given to you by your doctor. Instead, you "intoxicate" (*fill*) your mind with the spiritual truths from the Bible (not the facts from the doctor), and so begin to think you can "go to the other end of the bar" and whip the big bad cancer. The spiritual truth we need to be drinking in to intoxicate our natural-minded soul is- **Who his own self** (Jesus) **bare our sins in his own body on the tree, that we, being dead to sins, should live unto righteousness: by whose stripes ye** (all of us who will believe enough to receive it) **were**

healed. (Of all sickness, even cancer) (**1 Peter 2:24**). That healing cannot flow into our flesh or minds unless we get normal thinking out of the way and replace it with spiritual thinking. Which is faith, and faith comes natural to the born-again spirit mind. When this happens you begin to walk in the spirit, so lookout cancer!

That is what Paul is telling us in Ephesians 5:18. That we must be filled with the spirit to the point that our perception of this natural, carnal, fallen world around us is no match for our ability and power of the realm God lives in and tells us to walk in. Paul also tells us- ***This* I say then, Walk in the Spirit, and ye shall not fulfill the lust of the flesh (Gal-5:16).** Also in **Gal-5:25** we read- **If we live in the Spirit, let us also walk in the Spirit**. We see Jesus as the best example of someone doing this, our brains short circuit on this stuff, but our born again spirit man sees it as normal where it came from. Many people (*most*) have the mindset that "but that was Jesus" and "He could work miracles because He was God in the flesh." However, Paul himself and many others (*not just the apostles*) disproved this thinking by the very examples of miracles and power that accompanied their lives. When we saturate, or intoxicate, our souls and minds with what God says about us and our situation to the point that we *believe* what the Word says, we will no longer believe that the doctor's report is the final say in the matter. When we do that, we go back through the spiritual door that Adam closed for us, and enter through the one Jesus reopened. That spiritual door takes us into the good things that He has for us, and out of the bad that satan's system hands us. Jesus said- **I am the door: by me if any man enter in, he shall be saved, and shall go in and out, and find pasture (John 10:9).** We have already established that Jesus is The Word. If we speak His words about our mess, we are destroying the works of the devil- **He that committeth sin is of the devil; for the devil sinneth from the beginning. For this purpose, the Son of God was manifested, that he might destroy the works of the devil (1 John 3:8).** Whatever is bad in your life did not come from God, it is a result of the fall or directly caused by the camp of satan- **For we wrestle not against flesh and blood, but against principalities, against powers, against the rulers of the darkness of this world, against spiritual wickedness in high *places* (Eph. 6:12).** There is a dam called "unbelief" that holds

How God Got Mary Pregnant

back the power-flow of the Spirit realm. Once you get intoxicated with His ways, His thoughts, and His faith, all the religious "bar room" patrons that speak carnal-minded doubt doctrines to your emotions from many a pulpit each week will have to change their doctrine. Doctrine that stems from carnal thinking such as "I am a worm not a man", "just a lowly sinner saved by grace" will have no place in you. Their doctrine of doubt just will not have any effect on you or your thinking. Their doctrine is rooted in fear, which Jesus said not to have. I strongly suggest not waiting until cancer comes knocking at your door. Put into practice now, speaking His words to something that is not life threatening. That way you will have more of His mindset when/if something like cancer does come along. The religionist barroom patrons that have placed their bets against your success will lose the bet because they have not intoxicated themselves with His truths. This is not easy; it is VERY difficult. It is not difficult because God made it so, but only because it is so foreign to our carnal way of thinking. Our logical soul that loves dominance goes nuts trying to submit to this. We can overcome that kind of thinking by getting to know Him, and the first step in that process is to do the Romans 10:9-10 thing. The second step is to tell Him you want the Helper, the Teacher, the Holy Ghost (see John 14:26). Thirdly, get into His Word—the Holy Bible—and do not get your nose out of it….never.

I do want to caution you to not fall into the "health and wealth" doctrine taught by many TV preachers; what they teach is very close to this. All denominations have some truth in each of them. The health and wealth (mainly television preachers) crowd has been mockingly (by other competing groups) nicknamed the "blab it and grab it" or "name it and claim it" group, because of their similar teaching. I do have very serious issues with the perversion of scripture they have brought into Christendom that are dangerous. However, that does not take away from what the Bible teaches. Some churches and some well-known TV preachers have extracted a truth from scripture and perverted it to serve them. God did not come to start denominations that serve themselves. He came to re-start the family stolen from Him a long time ago. He wants you_____ (*do I need to say it again*) in that family.

He tells us to control our thought life by- **Casting down imaginations, and every high thing that exalteth itself against the knowledge of God, and bringing into captivity every thought to the obedience of Christ (II Cor. 10:5).** It is our perverted way of thinking that we are accustomed to (i. e. comfortable with because it comes natural) that stops faith from being developed. We are told- **Let this mind be in you, which was also in Christ Jesus (Ph. 2:5).** A mind that dwelt so much on the spirit that He knew how to walk in the spirit (*and on top of water*). If you will saturate yourself with His words, the hearing will change your mindset- **So then faith cometh by hearing, and hearing by the word of God (Romans 10:17).** When you cross that invisible bridge into the spirit arena of faith, then faith becomes present and faith is the substance that flows through into the kingdoms of men; lookout sickness! You need to get your soul to hearing His words, positive words, until they become faith-filled words. Think of it like this: The universe, every molecule, atom and sub-atomic particle, down to the Higgs field, came into being at His command. A command is words, words that He spoke. So, at the very core all created things can be manipulated by words in His name still today. Why? Because He gives us that authority in Jesus' name, for He qualified to take back the full authority Adam once had but lost due to his rebellion. It only works through faith and faith only comes by hearing and hearing of the Word.

I hope this book has been a blessing to you. If it leads you to accept our Lord's offer of salvation (*that would be the Romans 10:9-10 thing*) then it has done well. I know there is much more to the Bible that I do NOT know than what I do know. What I know today will change tomorrow. I, like all who seek, am growing in grace and knowledge (*that's my disclaimer*). I consider myself an elementary level teacher in the body of Christ (it is actually sad that the Church is in that condition). There are people out there that I learn from far better at this than I am. However, it takes all kinds, and maybe I will reach some that my mentors do not. In the editing process of this book, a younger editor questioned the wording of some of my paragraphs concerning spiritual concepts because it just does not make sense to our normal way of thinking, After reexamination I left them untouched. The young editor has never read that much of the Bible. An older editor, who has read it many times, had less or no trouble with the

How God Got Mary Pregnant

same paragraphs. So if you struggle with the concepts it is probably due to the same. Again, I say, read the Bible, it is the most important thing on earth! Jesus came that we may have life—real life—and not just on the other side in heaven but right here and now. The later part of John 10:10 again says- **I** (Jesus) **am come that they might have life, and that they might have *it* more abundantly.** Abundant can mean we can look each other up a trillion years from now and have tea, coffee together.

Printed in the USA
CPSIA information can be obtained
at www.ICGtesting.com
CBHW051751300724
12430CB00041B/580